act I "Orlando"

'16

Orlando

I.

I was alone. I was hiding in the attic. The head of a Moor swung from the rafters. The head was dry and the color and shape of an old ball. Two strands of hair stood in its left sunken cheek, hair coarse like that of a coconut. I was sixteen and dreamed of riding in fields of stone, of asphodel, fields watered by rivers. I dreamed of striking many heads of many colors off many shoulders, and bringing them back to hang from the rafters. My father said I was too young to ride with the armies in France. I practiced conquest with my blade in the attic. Sometimes I cut the cord and the skull bumped on the floor. When I hung it up again, my enemy grinned triumphantly through his shrunken, black lips and gently swung in the breeze. I was sixteen and in love with death, my own and those of my forebears who had come out of the northern mists wearing coronets on their heads. I loved solitary places, vast views, and the feeling of being for ever and ever and ever alone.

I was alone on top of a hill crowned by a single oak tree. My secret hiding place was so high up that I could see nineteen English counties and perhaps thirty or forty, if the weather was fine. Sometimes I could see the English Channel, wave reiterating upon wave. Rivers could be seen and pleasure boats and galleons setting out to sea, and armadas with puffs of smoke, and forts on the coast, and castles among the meadows. I saw my father's house; and my uncle's and the three great turrets that belonged to my aunt; and there their heath and the forest and the pheasant, the deer, the fox, the badger, and one day I fell. This is how my journey began. The hard root of the oak tree on which I had fallen became the back of a great horse, or the deck of a tumbling ship — it was anything to which I could attach my floating heart, the heart that tugged at my side, the heart that seemed filled with gales every evening when I walked out and climbed up to the oak tree on the summit. I tied my heart to the oak tree. The little leaves hung, the pale summer clouds stayed, my limbs grew heavy. I lay so quiet that by degrees the deer stepped nearer and the rooks wheeled and the swallows circled and the dragon flies shot past, as if the fertility of a summer's evening were woven around my body. The white clouds had turned red, the hills were violet, the woods purple, the valleys black and — this is how my journey began — a trumpet sounded. I was on my way.

The sound came from the valley, from my own great house in the valley that lost its darkness and became pierced with lights. The queen had come. I ran downhill and by shortcuts known only to me, I made my way through the vast congeries of rooms and staircases to the banqueting hall to sink upon my knees and offer a bowl of rose water to the great Queen herself.

I saw no more of her than her ringed hand in water. It was a memorable hand, a thin hand with long fingers always curling as if round orb or sceptre; a nervous, crabbed, sickly hand; a commanding hand, a hand that had only to raise itself for a head to fall; a hand attached to an old lady that smelt like a cupboard. The Queen's eyes were yellow. She always kept them wide open, they said, especially for shapely legs, violet eyes, hearts of gold, youth and innocence. She was growing old and worn and bent before her time. The sound of cannon was always in her ears. She saw always the glistening poison drop and the long stiletto. She listened, she dreaded — was that a curse, was that a whisper? The great rings flashed in the bowl and the Queen pressed my hair. Tradition says the Queen kissed me and I didn't know it, but she didn't forget me. Two years of quiet country life had not passed, and I had not written more than twenty tragedies and a dozen histories and a score of sonnets when a message came to attend the Queen at Whitehall.

"Here comes my innocent," she said. I wasn't. "Come," she said. She was sitting by the fire and looked me up and down. Eyes, mouth, nose, chest, hips, hands, I swear her lips twitched as her eyes ran over me. But when she looked at my legs she laughed out loud. I blushed. Instantly she plucked a ring from her swollen finger and bidding me bend my knee tied round it at the slenderest part the jewelled order of Knight of the Garter. Nothing after that was denied me.

act E
"orlando"

When the ocean winds delivered us from the Spaniards, when the guns were booming at the Tower and the air was thick enough with gunpowder to make one sneeze and the huzzas of the people rang beneath the windows, she pulled me down among the cushions and made me bury my face. She had not changed her dress for a month. I was half suffocated from the embrace. "This," she breathed, "this is my victory." A rocket roared up and dyed her old cheeks scarlet. She gave me land and houses. I was to be the son of her old age, the limb of her infirmity, the oak tree on which she leant her degradation. The Queen loved me.

But I was young. At that season of my life, when my head brimmed with rhymes and I never went to bed without striking off some conceit, the cheek of an innkeeper's daughter seemed fresher and the wit of the game keeper's niece seemed quicker than those of the ladies at Court. I began going frequently to disreputable places at night; wrapped in a gray cloak to hide the star at my neck and the Garter at my knee. There, with the mug before me, among the alleys and bowling greens, I listened to sailor's stories of horror on the Spanish main. I loved to hear them volley forth their songs while the parakeets pecked at the rings in their ears, and swore as vilely as their masters. The women perched on my knee, flung their arms round my neck, and guessing that something out of the common lay hid beneath my duffle cloak, were quite as eager to come to the truth of the matter as I was, but a nose can only be cut off in one way and maidenhood lost in another. (…)

"Orlando"
Act I

memory/cage

r

robert wilson

w

w

m

editions

PHOTOGRAPHS

BY VITTORIO SANTORO

TEXTS BY VIRGINIA WOOLF/DARRYL PINCKNEY/WOLFGANG
WIENS/ROBERT WILSON, HANS ARP, KURT SCHWITTERS,
THE BROTHERS GRIMM, JELALUDDIN RUMI, HENRIK IBSEN/
SUSAN SONTAG, HERMAN MELVILLE

PROLOGUE	5 minutes no text just music
ACT 1, SCENE A	12 minutes Man Text: Hans Arp, Konfiguration I, Konfiguration II
ACT 1, SCENE B	8 minutes Man Text: spoken or sung numbers
ACT 1, SCENE C	4 minutes Man Text: Hans Arp, Decisions in Dream
ACT 2, SCENE B	8 minutes (7 minutes music, 1 minute text in the end) Woman (possibility) Text: Kurt Schwitters, The Hand
ACT 2, SCENE C	4 minutes Child Text: Jakob and Wilhelm Grimm, The Louse and the Flea
ACT 2, SCENE A	12 minutes (music-text-music-text-music-text-music) Man (possibility) Text: Jean Arp, introduction to max ernst's natural history
ACT 3, SCENE C	4 minutes Child Text: Kurt Schwitters, Four Bear Songs, No. 3
ACT 3, SCENE B	12 minutes Woman Text: Else Lasker-Schüler, A song
ACT 3, SCENE A	8 minutes Woman and chorus Text: Lucretius, On the Nature of Things (Latin sung chorus and spoken in English)
ACT 4, SCENE A	6 minutes Hummed, sustained notes
ACT 4, SCENE B	6 minutes (Hummed, sustained notes leads to sung or spoken and then sung text) Woman Text: Jean Arp, The Seasons of the Clock the Strawberry the Velvety Animals and the Cradle
ACT 4, SCENE C	6 minutes (Sung text leads to chorus) Chorus Text: Lucretius, On the Nature of Things
EPILOGUE	5 minutes Child Text: Jakob and Wilhelm Grimm, The Ditmarsh Tale of Lies

.05

. 20

⅔ up
↑3 1,50

2,50

Prologue①

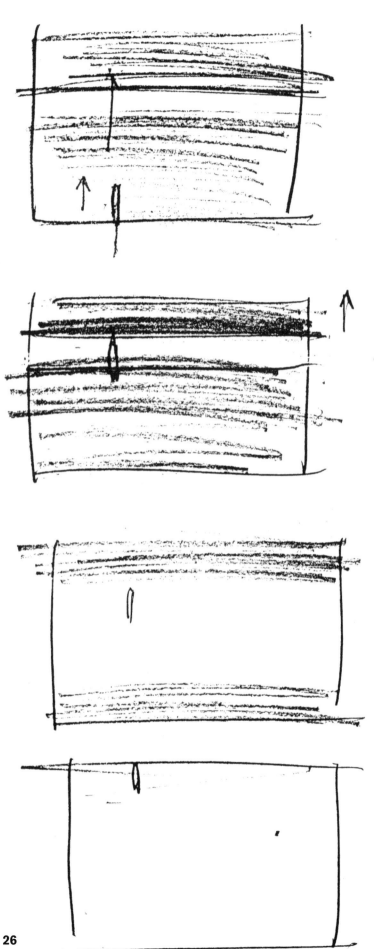

2.50

3.50

4.20

5.00

ACT 1, SCENE A

1

- das weiße haar der steine. das schwarze haar der wasser. das grüne haar der kinder. das blaue haar der augen.

- die wasser schließen ihre augen denn vom himmel fallen steine und kinder.

- den steinen den wassern den kindern und den augen fallen die haare aus.

- die steine haben in ihrer rechten hosentasche butter und in ihrer linken hosentasche brot und werden darum von jedermann hochachtungsvollst für butterbrote gehalten.

- die steinernen butterbrote tragen einen scheitel rechts die wasserigen butterbrote einen scheitel links und die kinderigen butterbrote einen scheitel in der mitte.

2

- solche geschichten kann man getrost der federflora erzählen

- selbst wenn einige kuttelkantige tische oder blumen mit scheuklappen darin vorkommen denn die steine sind analphabeten das wasser charakterlos und was nützt das flohgeheul der kinder das läusegedonner der augen.

- ihrer kraft bewusst nehmen die haare an den kuttelkantigen tischen platz.

- weiß schwarz grün und blau sind die farben des weltalls. man trägt jetzt grüne wiesen zu schwarzen schuhen und blauen haaren.

3

- die grünen wiesen. die blauen himmel. die schwarzen schuhe. die weißen haare.

- schwarze schuhe mit blauen lippen und blauen knöpfen.

- vierfarbige bärte in einer gestalt wie das lebende haar unserer zeit.

- blaue räume mit grünen schnäbeln und grünen schuhen.

- die kraft des löwen ist weiß.

4

- die kraft des feuers ist weiß.

- die treuen augen der kraft sind schwarz.

- schwarz ist das symbol für weiß.

- weiß bedeutet soviel wie auf wiedersehen oder wann werden wir wieder erwachen.

- antworten die weißen glocken mit ihrem grünen geläute auf die fragen der lippen oder auf die fragen der schnäbel.

5

- die feigheit der kraft ist schwarz wie die treuen augen der kraft.

- die vier farben der bärte sind weiß schwarz grün und blau.

- die schnelligkeit der steine ist blau.

- die charakterlosigkeit des wassers ist grün.

- das fleisch der kinder ist schwarz.

6

- das wasser schließt seine augen denn vom himmel fallen steine. die steine fallen auf die köpfe der kinder.

- den kindern fallen die augen aus. nun finden die kinder nicht mehr den weg von der decke in den mund und vom mund in den magen und vom magen in den topf.

- das blaue haar der steine ist gekämmt.

- das schwarze haar des wassers fällt in die suppe.

7

- unverzüglich machten sich die steine an die schwarze arbeit.
  grün strömte der schweiß von ihren blauen uhren und als es
  zwölf schlug waren die blauen himmel aufgeräumt und
  gereinigt.

- die schwarzen schuhe sind gewichst.
  die weißen haare sind gekämmt.

- mit charakterlosem wasser wuschen die steine die blutsprit-
  zer fort so daß alles schnell vergessen war und wieder von
  vorne angefangen werden konnte.

- das weiße haar der steine. das schwarze haar des wassers.
  das grüne haar der kinder. das blaue haar der augen.

8

- das weiße haar der steine. das schwarze haar der wasser.
  das grüne haar der kinder. das blaue haar der augen.

- das weiße haar. das schwarze haar. das grüne haar. das
  blaue haar.

- die steine. die wasser. die kinder. die augen.

- steinhaar. wasserhaar. kinderhaar. augenhaar.

- die grünen wiesen. die blauen himmel. die schwarzen schuhe.
  die weißen haare.

- blau grün schwarz feig und treu.

KONFIGURATION I
Hans Arp, 1930

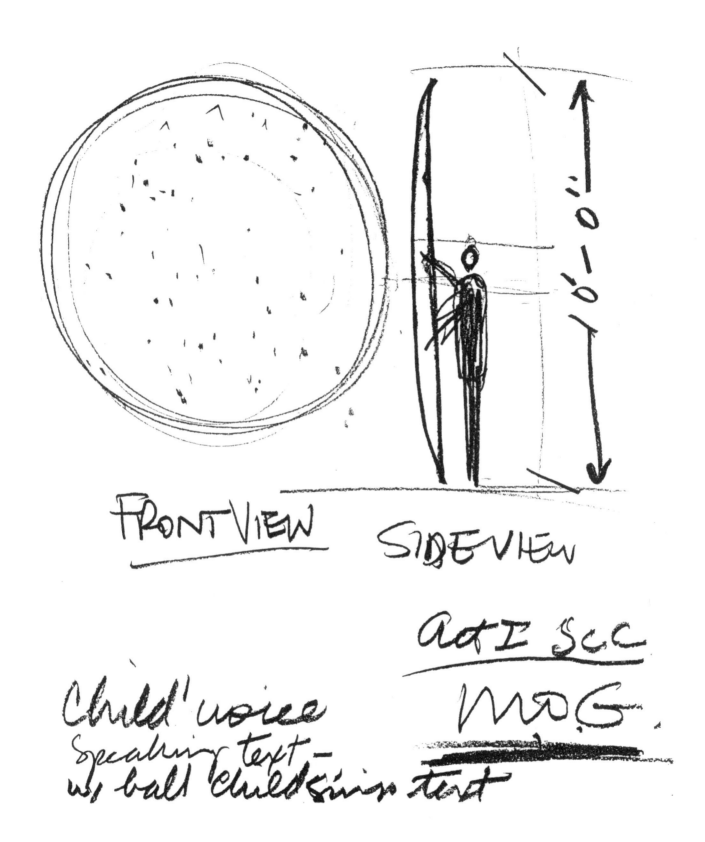

FRONT VIEW   SIDE VIEW

Act I sec

MOG.

Child'voice
Speaking text —
w/ ball children's text

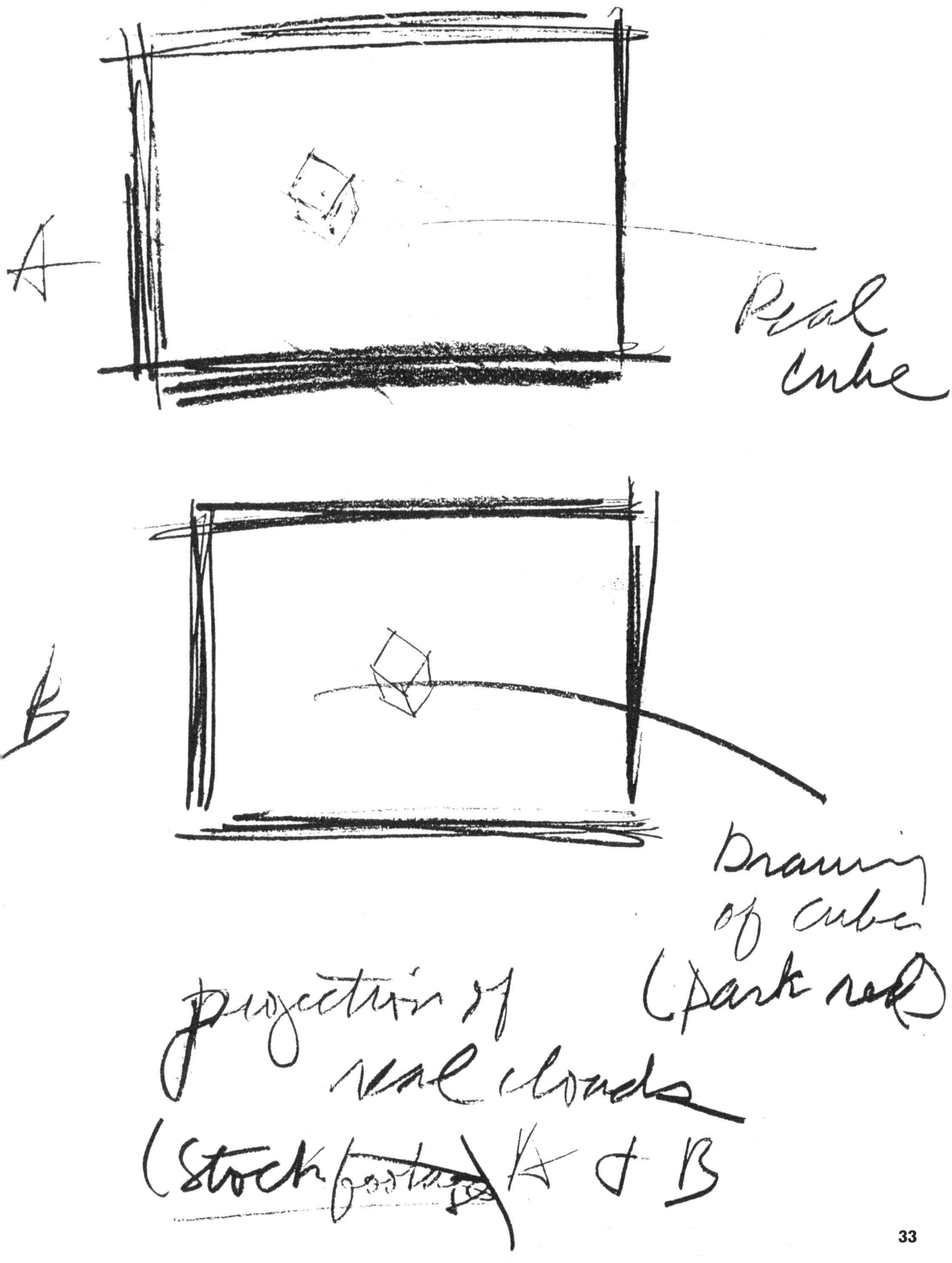

A

Real
cube

B

Drawing
of cubes
(Park red)

projection of
real clouds
(stock footage) A & B

33

ACT 2, SCENE C

Child's voice

A LOUSE AND A FLEA kept house together. They brewed their beer in an eggshell, and one day the louse fell in and got scalded. The flea began to scream at the top of his lungs. "Why are you screaming so?" asked the door. "Because Louse has got scalded." At that the door began to creak. A broom in the corner spoke up: " Why are you creaking, Door?" "Haven't I cause enough to creak?

> Louse has got scalded,
> Flea is crying."

At that the broom began to sweep furiously. A cart came along and said: "Why are you sweeping, Broom?" "Haven't I cause enough to sweep?

> Louse has got scalded,
> Flea is crying,
> Door is creaking."

"In that case, I'm going to run," said the cart, and he began to run furiously. He ran past the rubbish heap, and the rubbish heap said: "Why are you running, Cart?" "Haven't I cause enough to run?

> Louse has got scalded,
> Flea is crying,
> Door is creaking,
> Broom is sweeping."

"In that case I'm going to burn like mad," said the rubbish heap, and burst into a blaze. A tree, which was growing beside the rubbish heap, said: "Why are you burning, Rubbish Heap?" „Haven't I cause enough to burn?

> Louse has got scalded,
> Flea is crying,
> Door is creaking,
> Broom is sweeping,
> Cart is running."

"In that case I'm going to shake myself," said the tree, and shook himself so hard that all his leaves fell off. A girl who came out with her water pitcher saw him do it and said: "Tree, why are you shaking yourself?" "Haven't I cause enough to shake myself?

> Louse has got scalded,
> Flea is crying,
> Door is creaking,
> Broom is sweeping,
> Cart is running,
> Rubbish Heap is burning."

"In that case I'm going to smash my water pitcher," said the girl, and smashed her water pitcher. "Girl, why are you smashing your pitcher?" said the spring the water came from. "Haven't I cause enough to smash my pitcher?

> Louse has got scalded,
> Flea is crying,
> Door is creaking,
> Broom is sweeping,
> Cart is running,
> Rubbish Heap is burning,
> Tree is shaking himself."

"Goodness gracious," said the spring. "In that case I'm going to gush." And he began to gush furiously. And they were all drowned in the gushing water, the girl, the tree, the rubbish heap, the cart, the broom, the door, the flea, and the louse, the whole lot of them.

The Louse and the Flea
Jakob and Wilhelm Grimm, 1822

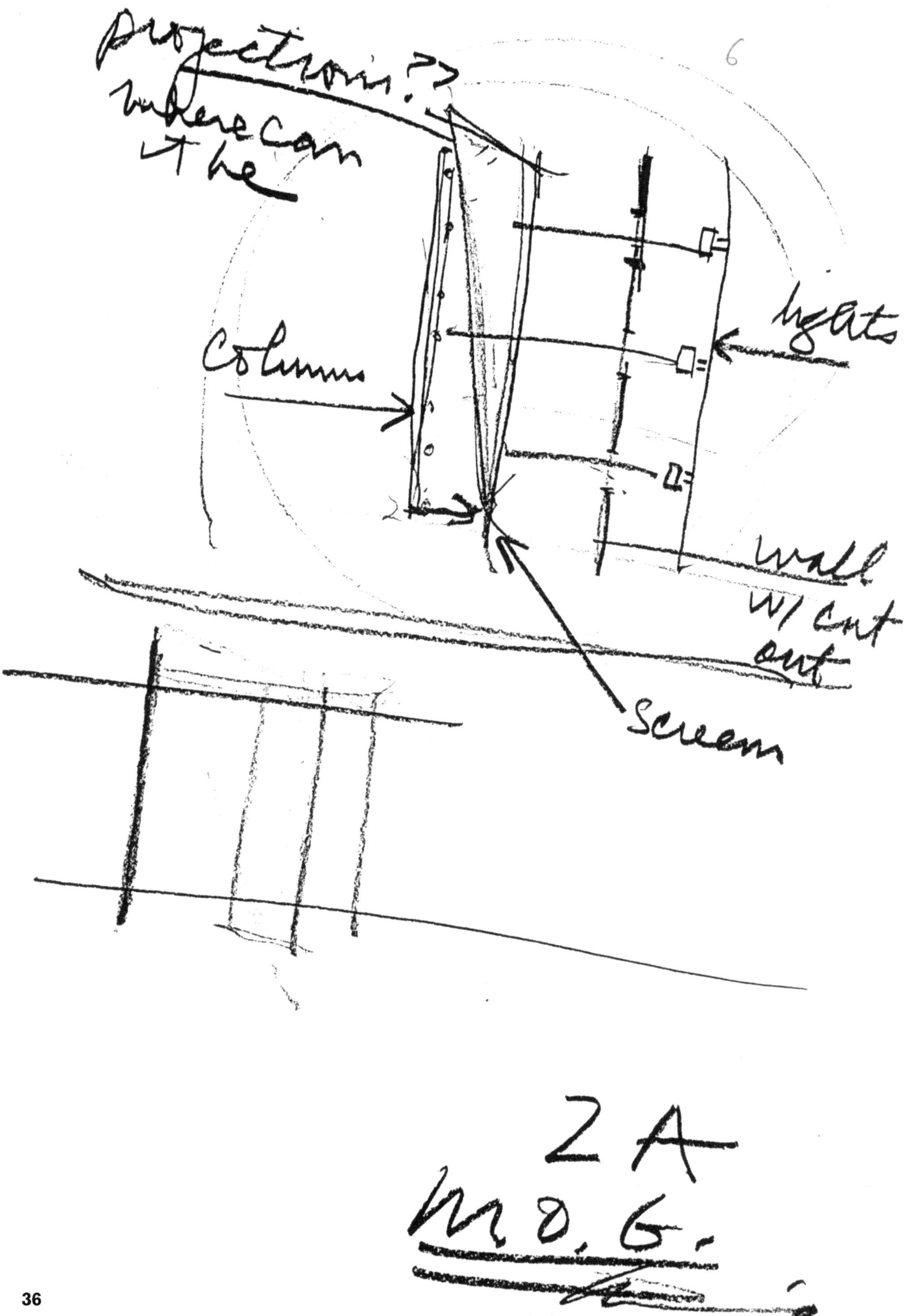

projection??
where can
it be

Column

lights

wall
w/ cut
out

Screen

Z A
M. O. G.

ACT 2, SCENE A

Man's voice (possibility)

Music

it is man who has replaced alarm-clocks by earthquakes showers of jordan almonds by showers of hail. the shadow of man encountering the shadow of a fly causes a flood. thus it is man who has taught horses to embrace one another like presidents kings or emperors sucking each other's beards licking each other's snouts plunging their tongues into patriotic profundities.

Music

Leaves never grow on the trees. like a mountain in bird's-eye view they have no perspective no soap no hybrid plastron no scotch cheeks no crypt. the spectator always finds himself in a false position before a leaf. he has the impression of carrying his head in his umbilicus his feet in his mouth his unwashed eyes in his hands.

Music

in the season of the harvest of conjugal diamonds huge cupboards with mirrors are found floating on their back in the oceans. the mirrors of these cupboards are replaced by waxed floors and the cupboard itself by a castle in spain. these mirrored cupboards are rented as rings to midwives and storks to make their innumerable rounds in and as tabourets to two gigantic rusty feet which rest upon them and sometimes tap a few steps pam pam.

enter the continents without knocking but with a muzzle of filigree.

Music

introduction to max ernst's natural history
Jean Arp, 1926

"Meder
ref. 2A
M.0,6.

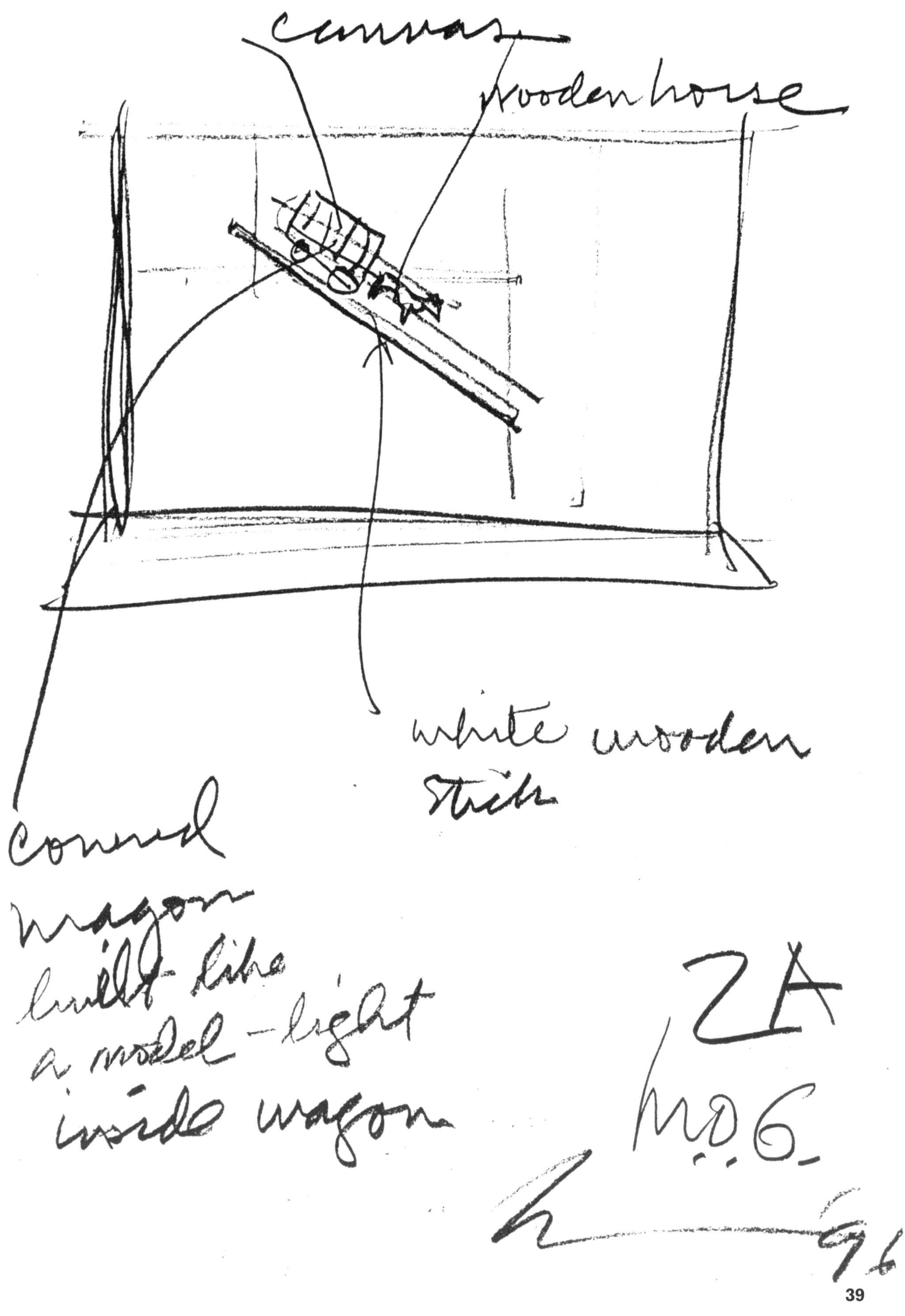

canvas

wooden house

white wooden
stick

covered
wagon
built like
a model - light
inside wagon

ZA
no. 6.

96

ACT 3, Scene C

Child's voice

How whacky is the bear, oh wow!
There do graze the sheep,
There does splash the water,
There do rush the fish,
There does dance the bear.
There do flash the rifles,
There does show his teeth.
There does smash the table,
There the bear does choke.
How whacky is his dance, oh wow!

Four Bear Songs, No. 3
Kurt Schwitters, 1928

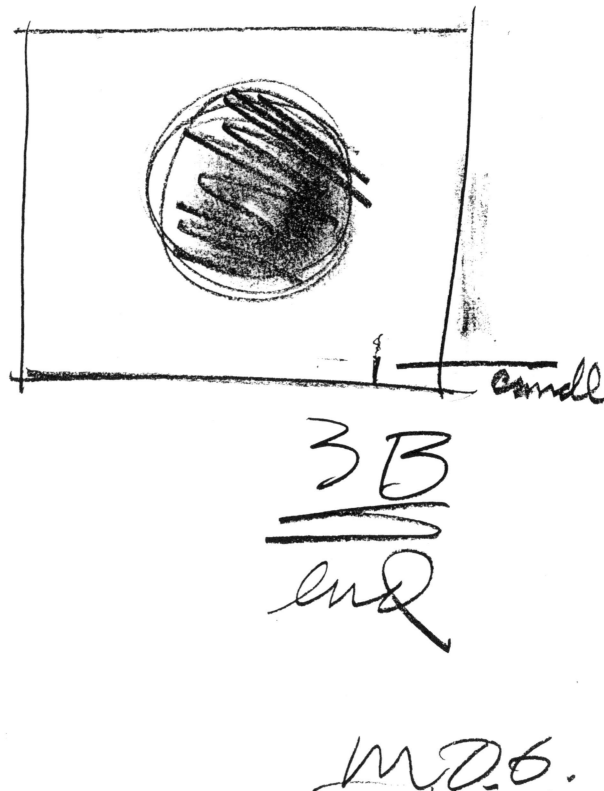

candle

$$\frac{3B}{end}$$

M.D.6.

Plan 4A

43

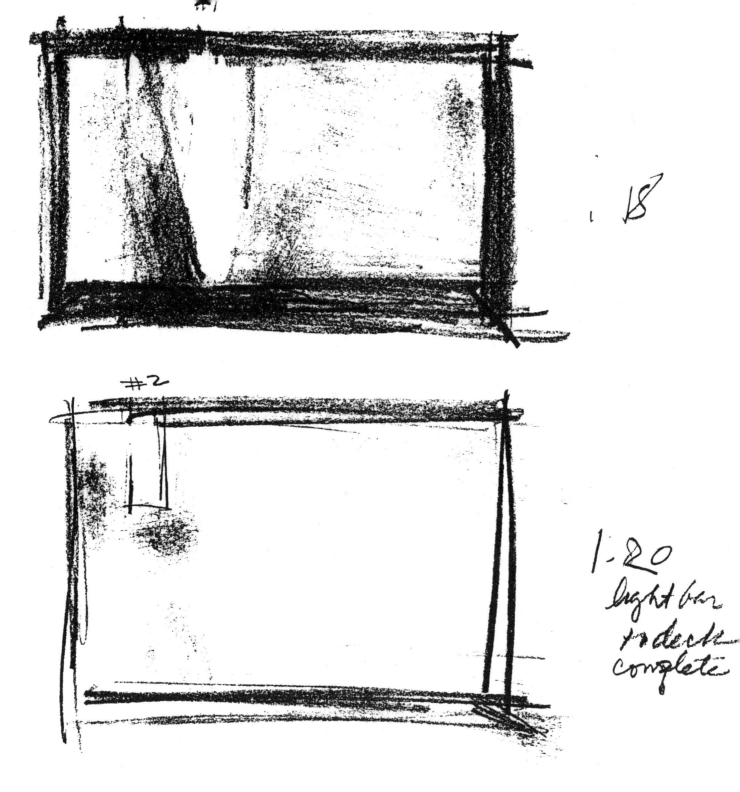

#2

1·80
light bar
to deck
complete

44

$$\frac{4A}{2084}$$

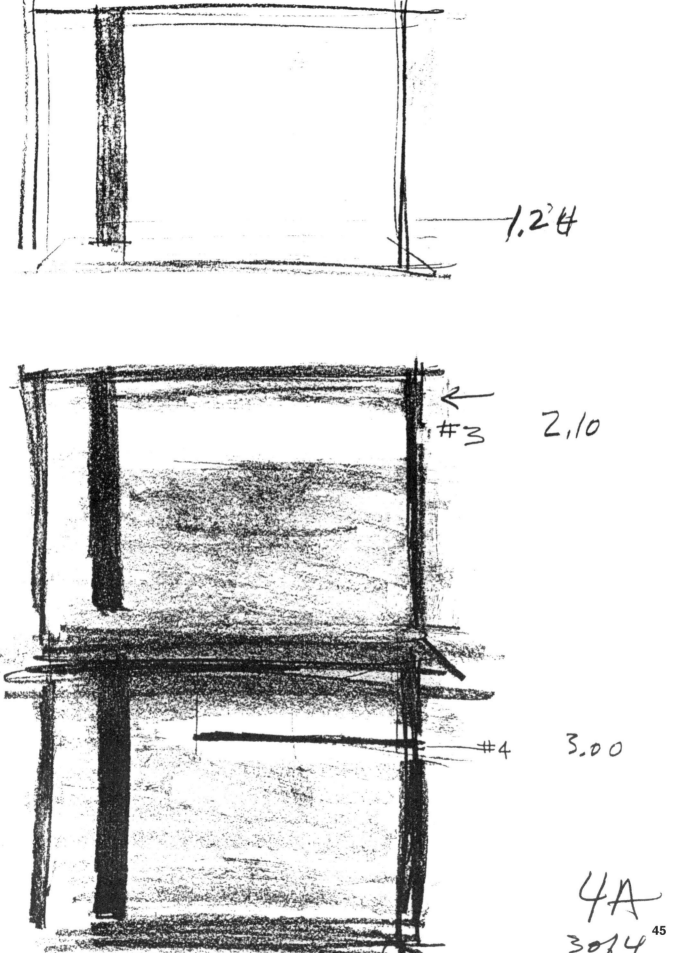

1.2' #

#3   2,10

#4   3.00

4A

30f4 45

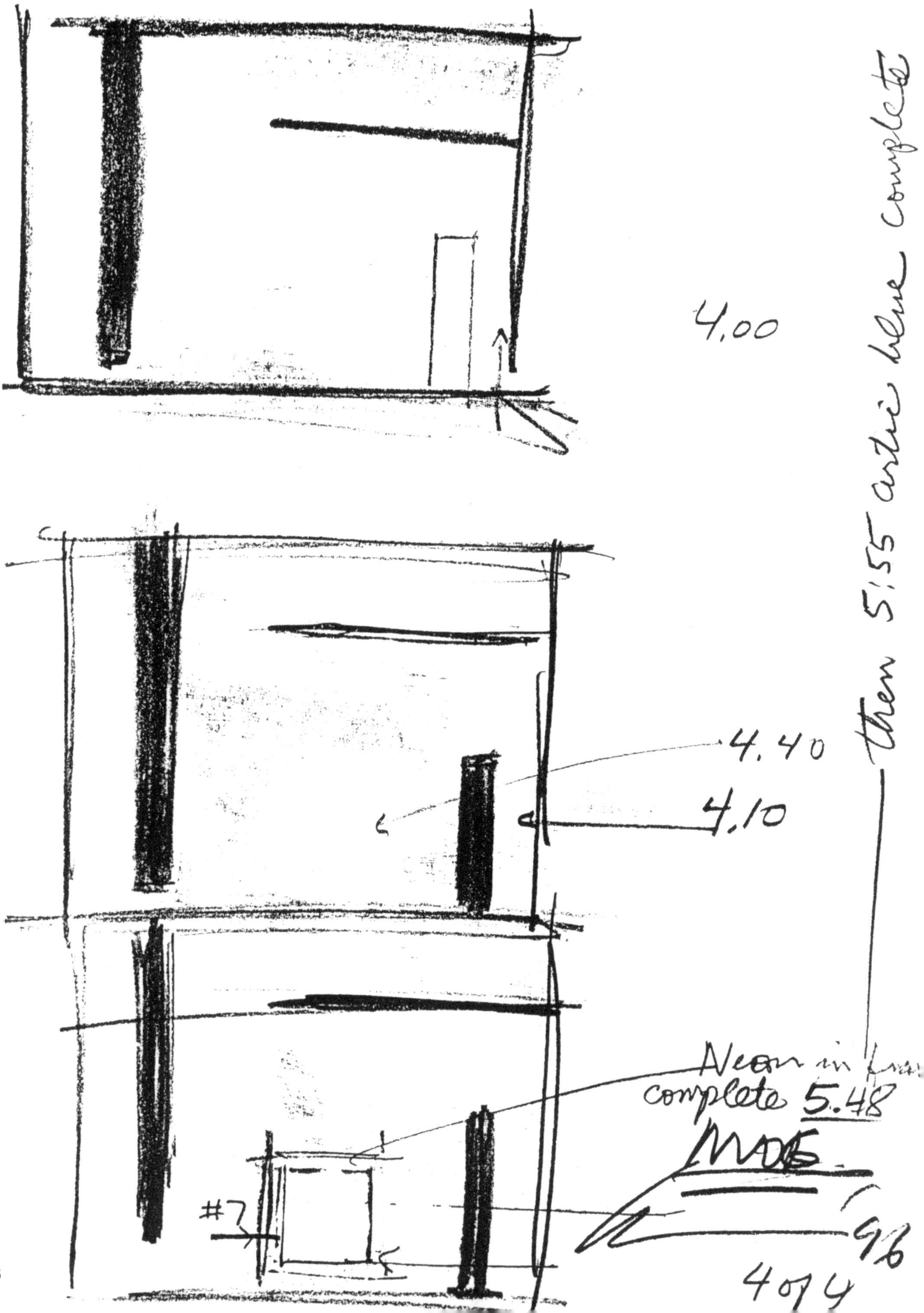

4.00

then 5:55 antie blue complete

.4.40

4.10

Neon in fram
complete 5.48

MADE

#7

96

4 of 4

EPILOGUE

Child's voice

I'm going to tell you something. I saw two roast chickens flying, they flew swiftly with their breasts turned heavenward and their backs hellward. An anvil and a millstone swam across the Rhine, as slowly and quietly as you please, and a frog was sitting on the ice at Whitsuntide, eating a plowshare. Three young fellows on crutches and stilts were trying to catch a hare. The first was deaf, the second was blind, the third was dumb, and the fourth couldn't move his feet. Do you want to know what happened? The blind one saw the hare running across the fields, the dumb one shouted to the lame one, and the lame one caught the hare by the collar. Some men wanted to sail on dry land. They set their sails in the wind and sailed across great fields. In the end they sailed over a high mountain and were miserably drowned. A crab was chasing a hare, and high up on the roof lay a cow, which had got there by climbing. In that country the flies are as big as the goats in this country. Open the window and let the lies out.

The Ditmarsh Tale of Lies
Jakob and Wilhelm Grimm, 1822

158
Out beyond ideas of wrongdoing and rightdoing,
there is a field. I'll meet you there.

When the soul lies down in that grass,
the world is too full to talk about.
Ideas, language, even the phrase *each other*
doesn't make any sense.

674
You don't have "bad" days and "good" days.
You don't sometimes feel brilliant and sometimes dumb.
There's no studying, no scholarly thinking having to do with love,
but there is a great deal of plotting, and secret touching,
and nights you can't remember at all.

64
When I die, lay out the corpse.
You may want ot kiss my lips,
just beginning to decay. Don't be frightened
if I open my eyes.

802
They say that Paradise will be perfect
with lots of clear white wine and all the beautiful women
since this is how it's going to be.

1319
We have a huge barrel of wine, but no cups.
That's fine with us. Every morning
we glow and in the evening we glow again.
They say there's no future for us. They're right.
Which is fine with us.

1794
At night we fall into each other with such grace.
When it's light, you throw me back
like you do your hair.

Your eyes now drunk with God,
mine with looking at you,
one drunkard takes care of another.

From "Odes" by Rumi

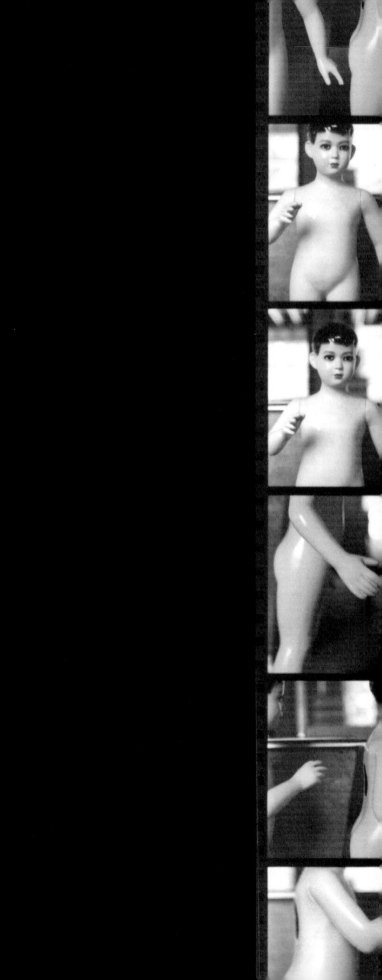

Orlando

II.

Your house is suddenly uninhabitable. Steps must be taken to end the matter instantly. You do what any other man would do and ask King Charles to send you as Ambassador Extraordinary to Constantinople.

You discharge your duties with admiration, have a finger in the most delicate negotiations between King Charles and the Sultan. Your days pass in a pleasant fashion. You rise about seven, wrap yourself in a long Turkish cloak and light a cheroot. You are entranced with the city beneath you. The mist lies so thick that the domes of Santa Sofia seem to be afloat. Uncovered there is a river, there the Galata Bridge, and there the green turbanned pilgrims without eyes or noses, begging alms, there the pariah dogs picking up shit, the shawled women, the innumerable donkeys, men on horses carrying long poles. Soon the whole town is astir with the beating of gongs, cryings to prayer, lashing of mules, and rattle of brass-bound wheels, while sour odors, made from bread fermenting and incense, and spice, rise to the heights of Pera itself.

Later, properly scented, curled, and anointed, you receive visits from secretaries and other high officials carrying, one after another, red boxes which yield only to one golden key. Within are papers of the highest importance, papers that require wax and seals until luncheon, a splendid meal of thirty courses. After luncheon, lackeys announce that a coach and six are at the door and you go, preceded by purple Janissaries running on foot and waving great ostrich feather fans above their heads.

They are saying that you are in the prime of life, with the power to stir the fancy and rivet the eye and the power is a mysterious one compounded of beauty, birth, and some rarer gift, which, to have done with it, is called glamour. A million candles are burning in you without your having the trouble of lighting a

single one. You move like a stag. Rumors gather round you. Shepherds, gipsies, donkey drivers, men, women, sing songs about he who drops his emeralds in a well. You have no friends, no attachments, and attend to your duties so indefatigably that you have not been at the Horn more than two years before King Charles signifies his intention of raising you to the highest rank in the peerage.

The patent of nobility arrives in a frigate at the end of the great fast of Ramadan and you host an entertainment more splendid than any that has been known before or since in Constantinople. The night is fine, the crowd immense, and the windows of the Embassy are brilliantly illuminated. Inside, pyramids of ice, fountains of negus, jellies made to represent His Majesty's ships, swans made to represent water lilies, birds in golden cages, gentlemen in slashed crimson velvet, ladies' headdresses at least six foot high, musical boxes, oceans to drink, and as the clock strikes twelve you appear on the center balcony which is hung with priceless rugs. Six Turks of the Imperial Body Guard, each over six foot in height, hold torches on either side. Rockets rise in the air, shouts go up from the people. You are kneeling. An admiral places the Collar of the Most Noble Order of the Bath around your neck, then pins the Star to your breast. Another gentleman of the diplomatic corps places on your shoulders the ducal robes and hands, on a crimson cushion, the ducal coronet. You are taking the golden circlet of strawberry leaves to put on your head. Either the people are expecting a miracle, a shower of gold from the sky, or it is a signal chosen for an attack to begin. Bells begin to ring, the harsh cries of the prophets are heard above the shouts of the people, many fall flat to the ground and touch the earth with their foreheads. A door bursts open. Women shriek, people press into the banqueting rooms, someone seizes a candelabra and dashes it to the ground. An admiral orders the bugles to be sounded, a hundred soldiers instantly stand at attention, and soon the embassy is empty of company, shut up by 2 a.m. You are seen to go to your room, still wearing the insignia of your rank, and shut the door. You are heard to lock it, which is against custom.

The next morning you are a duke and your secretaries find you sunk in a profound slumber amid bed clothes that are much tumbled. The room is in some disorder, your coronet has rolled on the floor, your cloak and garter are in a

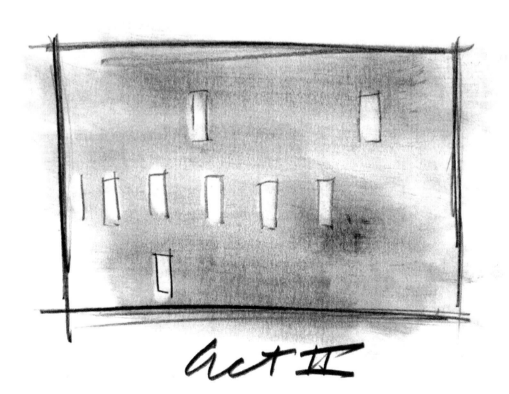

Act II

heap on a chair. The table is littered with papers. By afternoon a doctor is summoned. He applies plasters, nettles, emetics, but without success. You sleep on.

On the seventh day of your trance, the first shot of a terrible and bloody insurrection is fired. The Turks are rising against the Sultan, setting fire to the town, and putting every foreigner they can find either to the sword or to the bastinado. Some gentlemen of the British Embassy are swallowing keys rather than let their secrets fall into the wrong hands. The rioters are breaking into your room. Seeing you stretched out, they think you are dead, and only rob you of your coronet and robes.

You are alone. You are waking. You are stretching yourself. You are standing upright. You take a bath. You have become a woman, there is no denying it. But in every other respect you remain as you have been. The change of sex, though it alters the future, does nothing to alter identity. Your memory goes back through all the events of your past life without encountering any obstacle. You wash and dress in Turkish coats and trousers which may be worn by either sex. You consider your position. You can scream, ring the bell, or faint, but you are not surprised. You have awakened in a position delicate for a young lady of rank. You stick a pair of pistols in your belt. You wind strings and strings of emeralds and pearls through your costume. You lean out the window, whistle, descend the littered, shattered, bloodstained staircase to a giant fig tree where an old gipsy on a donkey waits. You are leaving Constantinople.(…)

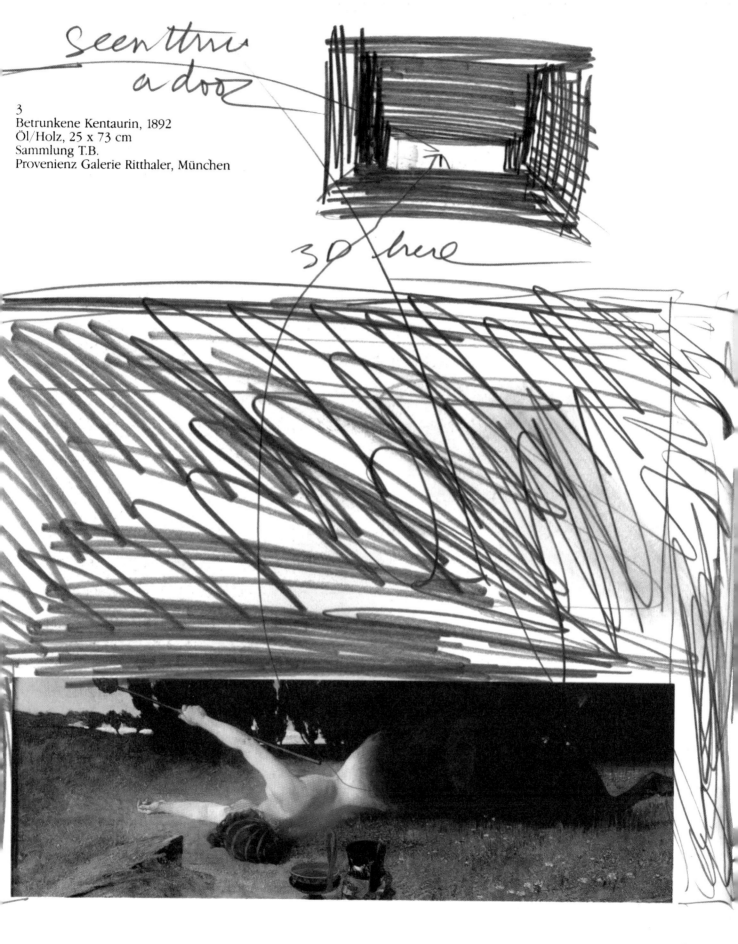

3
Betrunkene Kentaurin, 1892
Öl/Holz, 25 x 73 cm
Sammlung T.B.
Provenienz Galerie Ritthaler, München

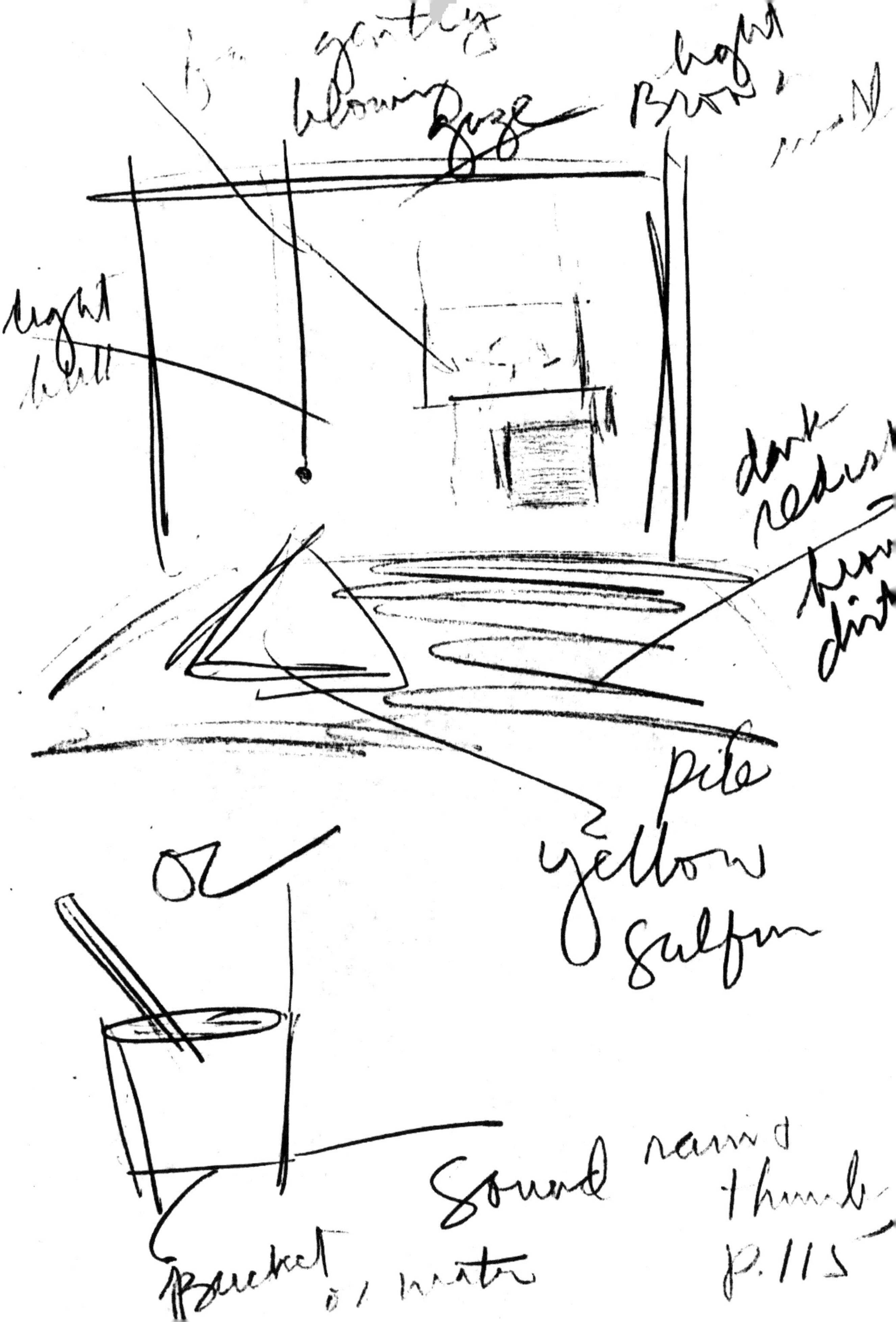

gently

blowing Buye

light Brown

light
lidle

dark
redish

brown
dirt

pile
yellow
Sulfur

oz

bucket
o/ water

Sound raining
Thumb
p.115

photo reproduction

photo reprod...

vase

white fig

whisper text

...ry oder Franz von Stuck
(zugeschrieben)
MIT DUNKLEM HUT
1915 (Kat. 236)

Mary Toehler

reproduced on silk

w/ a fan blowing the silk

MARY TOCHTER VON FRANZ VON STUCK   115

12 Schmoll 1968, S. 72.

13 Information aus der Familie (13. Dezember 1993, seine Anm. 9).

14 Barbara Hardtwig meint, daß Franz von Stuck, entsprechend den Sitten und moralischen Maßstäben seiner Zeit, seine Frau nicht als Objekt der Erotik dargestellt sehen wollte. Es kann aber auch sein, daß Franz von Stuck weniger mit der Kamera vertraut war oder, daß die Bilder mit Selbstauslöser angefertigt wurden.

15 Barbara Hardtwig vermutet, daß diese Aktaufnahmen auch während sogenannter Herrenabende in der Villa Stuck gemacht wurden. Siehe Franz von Stuck: Bestandskatalog des Museums Villa Stuck, 1996.

16 Einer der sehr wenigen zeitgenössischen Berichte darüber stammt von dem Bildhauer Richard Knecht (1887–1966), der über seine Erlebnisse beim Aktformen der großen Plastik Amazone schrieb »Auch seine Frau kam öfter ins Atelier. Dann war es allerdings mit der Ruhe vorbei. Sie hatte eine hohe, schrille Stimme, wenn sie rief: ›Wunderbar, wunderbar, du bist ein Genie‹ Stuck gab meistens gar keine Antwort.« Obermeier 1976, S. 222. Freundlicher Hinweis: Barbara Hardtwig.

17 Information aus der Familie (13. Dezember 1993, siehe Anm. 9).

18 Mary Hoose, »... seit den neunziger Jahren als leuchtender Stern in den großen Münchner Salons der ... der Künstlerschaft«. Georg Jakob Wolf, Die Münchnerin. Künstler- und Sittenbilder aus dem alten München. München 1924, S. 199, zitiert von Christine Hoh-Slodczyk in Poetter 1984, S. 118. Vgl. das 1894 entstandene Porträt von Mary Lindpaintner als Salome von Franz von Lenbach. In: Golleck 1987, S. 23?...

19 Freundlicher Hinweis: Barbara Hardtwig. Siehe Franz von Stuck: Bestandskatalog des Museums Villa Stuck, 1996.

20 Einige der Ausnahmen sind die photographierten Porträts von Martha Butzer und Erna Bohneward zwischen 1921 und 1923. Die Zahl von Gemälden aus dieser Zeit ist auch geringer.

21 wie Anm. 19.

22 Im Besitz des Munch-Museet, Oslo.

26 [...]
[...] Photographie und Dialog im Dialog von 1890 bis heute [...]
[...] Kunsthaus Zürich, 1977 und Das Selbstporträt im Zeitalter der [...]
Photographie. Maler und Photographen im Dialog von sich selbst (Hrsg. Erika [...]
Billeter), Kunstverein Freiburg/Breisgau und Kunsthalle, 1985

Mary oder Franz Stuck (zugeschrieben)
Lydia Fez (Venetia), undatierte Aufn., 1900
(Kat. [...] und 17)

image
see thru
a partially
opened
door

365
Der Nibelungen Not, um 1920
Öl/Holz, 98 x 41,2 cm
Privatbesitz

Maybe
13 small
w/ landscape
or only
it will

built This image
built 3-D

34
Frühling, um 1920
Öl/Leinwand, 34,5 x 31,3 cm
Privatbesitz

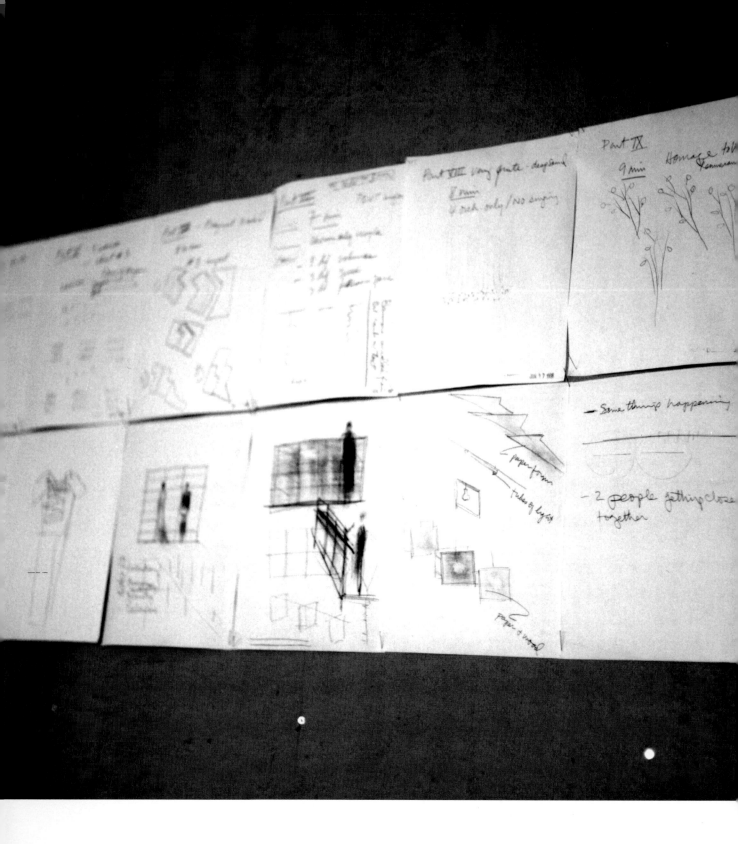

Scene from **THE LADY FROM THE SEA**

by Susan Sontag

(based on the play by
Henrik Ibsen)

ELLIDA to audience:

Seals are actually people who of their own free will have plunged into the
ocean and drowned. Once each year, on Twelfth Night, they get a chance
to take off their sealskins, and then they look just like everyone else.

HARTWIG (her husband):

I don't believe this story.

ELLIDA:

Until dawn, when they must return to their seal form, they dance and
play on the flat rocks by the shore and in the breeding caves near the
beach, and they have a marvelous time.

HARTWIG:

Fornicating. Like animals.

ELLIDA:

There was a boy from the southmost farm in Mikladalur who heard people say
that the seals got together on Twelfth Night in a cave on the breeding
grounds not far from the village. So, that evening, he went there to
see if it was true. He hid behind a rock in front of the cave. After the
sun went down, he saw seals swimming from all directions toward the spot
he was crouching. When they reached the shore, they took off their skins
and put them on a flat rock on the beach. He could hardly believe his
eyes. They did look just like ordinary people!

HARTWIG:

Nonsense! Folklore!

ELLIDA:

The boy was fascinated with these creatures. Ordinary people! Fat and
thin. Old and young. Tall and short. Ordinary except for one.

HARTWIG:

Ahhhh…

ELLIDA:

For then he saw the most beautiful woman he had ever seen step out of a
sealskin. He watched where she placed her skin, which wasn't far from
the rock behind which he was crouching. The boy crept over and took it
and returned to his hiding place.

HARTWIG:

She insists on telling this story.

ELLIDA:

The seal folk danced all night long, but when it started to grow light
they returned to their skins. The beautiful seal woman could not find
hers and wrung her hands and wailed because the sun was about to come up.
But just before it did, she caught its scent near the hiding place of the
boy from Mikladalur. She pleaded with him to give it back to her. But he
walked away from her, and she had to follow him. All the way to the
farm.

HARTWIG:

You see what's going to happen.

"The Lady From the Sea"

'96

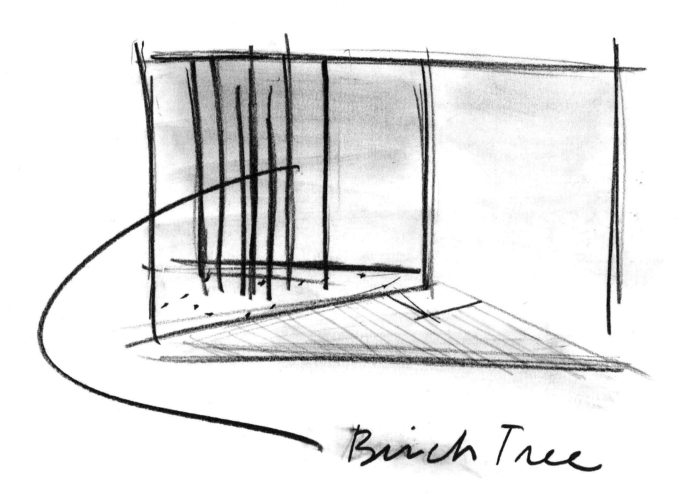

Birch Tree

L. F.S.

BIRCH
TREES
that
fly
m

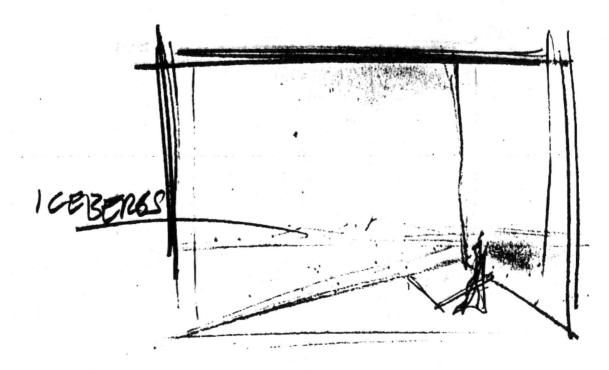

ICEBERGS

ELLIDA:

Into the house. Into his bed.

To make her into an ordinary woman. To make himself into a man.

He took her to be his wife. And they got on well together. They had
children. She loved him. She loved their children, especially the
first-born, a little boy with strange blueish-white eyes. But the
husband had to be careful not to let her get to her sealskin. He kept it
in a locked chest and always carried the key with him.

HARTWIG:

Now something sad happens. Inevitably. The man from Mikladalur was happy
with his seal wife. Happiness has to end.

ELLIDA:

One day he went fishing, and while he was sitting out at sea, pulling in
fish, his hand happened to brush his belt where the key usually hung. He
was dumbfounded to realize that he must have forgotten the key at home.
In his grief he cried out: "This evening I'll be without a wife." The
other fishermen pulled in their lines and rowed home as fast as they
could. When the man from Mikladalur got to his house, his wife was gone.
Only the children were there sitting quietly. So that they would not hurt
themselves while they were alone in the house, his wife had put out the
fire and locked up all the knives and sharp objects.

HARTWIG:

How considerate of her!

ELLIDA:

She had indeed found the key and opened the chest, and when she saw the
sealskin, she had to take it, after which she had run down to the beach,
pulled on her sealskin, and plunged into the sea. This is where the old
saying comes from: "He couldn't control himself any more than a seal that

finds its skin."
HARTWIG:

Couldn't control herself? She didn't really love him, that's all.

ELLIDA:

When she leaped into the sea, her seal mate found her, and they swam
away together. All these years he had been waiting for her to come back
to him.

HARTWIG:

You see! She'd never loved her husband!

ELLIDA:

When the children she had with the man from Mikladalur went down to the
beach, a seal could be seen just off the shore watching them, and
everyone thought it was their mother.

WANGEL:

She never loved her children either!

ELLIDA (addressing Hartwig directly for the first time):

How can you contradict a legend?

HARTWIG:

Cold. Like the sea.

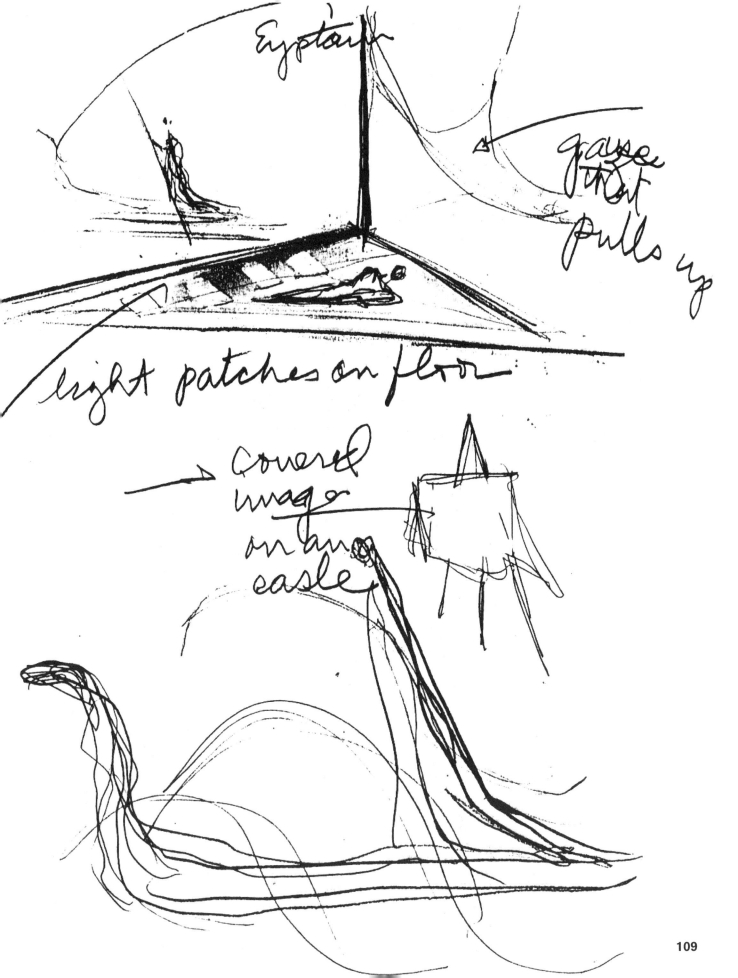

Explain

gaze that pulls up

light patches on floor

Covered image on an easle

The Lady From the Sea

'96

Orlando

III.

(…) My ankle is broken. The birds say follow us to the rim of the world and there drink forgetfulness. Forget the tough heather roots that trip women. I cannot rise. Here I am content, with the scent of the bog myrtle and the meadow-sweet in my nostrils. I have found my mate. I am nature's bride. Here will I lie in the cold embraces of the grass. I have found a greener laurel. My forehead will be cool always. These are wild birds' feathers, the owls, the nightjars. I shall dream wild dreams. My hands shall wear no wedding ring. The roots shall twine about my fingers. I have sought happiness through many ages and not found it; fame and missed it; love and not known it; life, and behold, death is better. I have known many men and many women. None have I understood. It is better that I should lie at peace here with only the sky above me, as the gipsy in Turkey told me years ago. The clouds churn themselves into a marvelous golden foam. I see a track in it, and camels passing single file through the rocky desert among red dust. I hear goat bells ringing, a gun far out at sea. That's the Armada. No, it's Admiral Nelson. No, those wars are over. I hear something in the ground, something deep within. A hammer or an anvil. Or is it a heart beating? Tick-tock, tick-tock, it hammers, it beats, the heart in the middle of the earth and becomes the trot of a horse. One, two, three, four, and then it stumbles, a twig cracks, the hoofs suck the wet bog. It is a horse. Towering dark against the plovers and yellow sky of dawn, I see a man on horseback. "Madam," he says, "you're hurt." "Sir, I am dead."

(…) I listen to voices from America, I see men fly, I rise through the air, and all the smells of the world cling to the first floor.

Time has passed over me. This is the oncome of middle age. Nothing is any

longer one thing. I take up a handbag, someone lights a pink candle, and I see a girl in Russian trousers. When I step outside I hear goat bells. I see mountains. When I drive my head is full of mountains.

Here is a market, here is a funeral. Here is a procession with banners. The body and mind are like scraps of torn paper tumbling from a sack and the process of motoring out of London resembles the chopping up into small pieces of body and mind, which precedes unconsciousness and perhaps even death. At last the little bits fall more slowly. Separate scraps now turn over by themselves in the air, each one a particular self. But it is not plain sailing. The self I call for does not come forth. These selves of which we are built up, one on top of the other, as plates are piled on a waiter's hand, have attachments elsewhere, sympathies, little constitutions and rights of their own, so that one will only come if it is raining, another in a room with green curtains, another if Mrs. Jones is not there and another if you can promise it a glass of wine, for everybody can multiply the different terms which his different selves have made with him. All right then. I have a variety of selves to call upon. The boy who sat on the hill, the boy who handed the Queen the bowl of rose water, the young man who fell in love with Sasha, the ambassador, or the girl among the gipsies, the woman who called Mar for hot baths and evening fires, or Shelmerdine for crocuses in autumn woods or Bonthrop for the death we die daily. I can change selves as quickly as I drive. There's a new one at every corner. The one I need most keeps aloof, the conscious self, which is the uppermost and has the power to desire, as happens when it wishes to be nothing but one self. This is what some call the true self, compact of all selves within us, commanded and locked up. I fling after it words like nets which shrivel as I've seen nets shrivel drawn on deck with only sea weed in them. Sometimes there's an inch of silver in the bottom of the net. But never the great fish who lives in the coral groves.

All is contained as water is contained by the sides of a well. So now am I dark, still, a single self, my real self. Here are the beech trees and oak trees, the deer with its horns caught in wire netting. Here is the courtyard where hundreds of years ago I came on horseback or in a coach, with men riding before or coming after, where plumes tossed, torches flashed. The rooms of the house

Act IV

Act III "Orlando"

brighten. They have nothing to conceal from me. We have been together for so long.

I came to these rooms as a child, as a man, crying and dancing. In this window seat I had Spanish wine, in that chapel I was married. My soul will come and go for ever with the reds on the panels and the greens on the sofa. Rows of chairs with all their velvets stand ranged against the wall holding out their arms for Elizabeth, but no queen or king will ever sleep here again. "Please do not touch," the printed notices say. The house is past the touch and control of the living.

Night comes, night that I love of all times, night in which the reflections in the dark pool of the mind shine more clearly than by day. It is not necessary to die in order to look deep into the darkness where things shape themselves. There is my husband's brig, rising to the top of the wave. Up it goes, up, up. The white arch of a thousand deaths rises before it, and then the wind sinks, the waters grow calm, the waves move in the moonlight. I have forgotten my name and I am standing by an oak tree. Beautiful, glittering names fall out of the sky like a steel blue feather. I see them fall, turning like a slow arrow. He is coming, as he always came, in moments of dead calm, when the wave rippled and the spotted leaves fell slowly over my foot in the autumn wood; when the leopard in the attic was still. The moon is on the water, but nothing moves between sky and sea. Will he come? A great house waits with its windows robed in silver, lit for the coming of a dead Queen. I see dark plumes tossing in the courtyard, and torches flickering. The cold breeze of the present brushes my face with its little breath of fear. But I am alone.

Virginia Woolf's **Orlando**

Extracted and arranged by
Darryl Pinckney, Wolfgang Wiens and Robert Wilson

A British Outsider Embraced With a French Blockbuster

By ALAN RIDING

PARIS, July 9 — Like many other cities, Paris now routinely uses blockbuster shows to revive interest in artists ranging from Poussin to Cézanne. But what distinguishes the major retrospective of Francis Bacon that just opened at the Georges Pompidou Center is that the British artist died only four years ago. Already, it seems, his work is considered ripe to be rediscovered.

Not that Bacon lacked for attention in his lifetime. In fact, one of the most important exhibitions of his works was held at the Grand Palais in Paris in 1971. France nonetheless always viewed him as something of an outsider, a figurative painter when abstract and then Conceptual Art were all the rage, a man whose distinct visual language seemed to owe nothing to French artistic tradition.

For a new generation, then, the show at the Pompidou Center, the largest Bacon exhibition in a decade, is indeed a discovery. And it has been received here as such, with extensive coverage in newspapers and magazines and the publication of a comprehensive 356-page catalogue. The exhibition, which closes on Oct. 14, has 79 paintings, including 16 of Bacon's 30 triptychs, and 7 works on paper.

"Bacon at last!" Jean-Marie Tasset wrote in Le Figaro. "If he had not been a millionaire, he would no doubt have been our martyr of contemporary art. For so long he was scorned as reactionary and conventional by the official thinkers of the day. Long excluded, he is now recognized by all. Through his life and work, Bacon showed that individual courage is the best way of fighting prejudice."

Bacon made no effort to reach out to most of his contemporaries. For many years he was a close friend of the painter Lucian Freud, although he disliked being grouped with Mr. Freud, Leon Kossoff, Frank Auerbach, R. B. Kitaj and Michael Andrews in a so-called School of London. He also dismissed Jackson Pollock and Willem de Kooning and made no secret of his deep distaste for the whole range of nonfigurative postwar art movements.

What becomes apparent in this exhibition is that from the moment he created his "Three Studies for Figures at the Base of a Crucifixion" in 1944, Bacon found his own tormented vision of art. And until his death in 1992 at the age of 82, he continued to explore the disturbingly deformed images of the human face and body that distinguish his work from anything before or since. His favorite subject in his later years was John Edwards, the friend to whom he left $16.9 million. Bacon liked to consider the 1944 triptych,

with its monstrous semi-human figures set against an acid orange background, as marking the start of his career as an artist. In truth, he began drawing and painting more than 15 years earlier, but he destroyed almost everything he did. Of 10 surviving pre-1944 paintings, three are in the show here, including his ghostly "Crucifixion" of 1933, which was well received at the time.

Bacon was born in Dublin of English parents in 1909 and moved with his family to London in 1914. In 1925, at 16, he left home after a fight with his father and began what became an infamously bohemian life. He began work as a decorator and furniture designer and often went to Europe. In 1926, he visited a Picasso exhibition in Paris that inspired him to start drawing.

By the mid-1930's, he had given up decorating for

Bacon was a figurative painter in a sea of abstract and Conceptual artists.

painting but had had little success. He showed his work in some collective exhibitions and did odd jobs to make ends meet. The two other early works on display here point the way to his lifelong use of rich, almost garish colors, although their styles are derivative, "Interior of a Room" (1935) of post-Cubism and "Figures in a Garden" (1936) of Surrealism. Two of the works on paper, one an hommage to Picasso, also date to this period.

In 1944, recognition of Bacon as an original began to grow. His personal life was tumultuous: he was an inveterate gambler, he always drank heavily and he flaunted his homosexuality. But his provocative way of life seemed to inspire him to create. He was an avowed atheist, yet he returned frequently to the theme of crucifixion, always calling his works "studies," as if one day he planned to paint a complete

Continued on Page C20

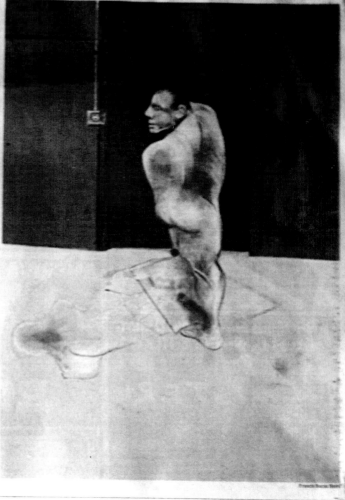

Francis Bacon's "Study for a Portrait of John Edwards" (1986), who was the artist's favorite subject in his final years and whom he left $16.9 million when he died in 1992.

...itish Outsider Embraced
...a French Blockbuster

ALAN RIDING

— Like many other cities, Paris ...lockbuster shows to revive inter... from Poussin to Cézanne. But ...e major retrospective of Fran... ...pened at the Georges Pompidou ...itish artist died only four years ..., his work is considered ripe to

...lacked for attention in his life. ...e most important exhibitions of ...t the Grand Palais in Paris in ...eless always viewed him as ...ider a figurative painter when ...ceptual Art were all the rage, a ...visual language seemed to owe ...tistic tradition.

...ration, then, the show at the ...largest Bacon exhibition in a ...covery. And it has been re..., with extensive coverage in ...zine and the publication of a ...ge catalogue. The exhibition ..., has 79 paintings, including 16 ..., and 7 works on paper.

...Jean-Marie Tasset writes in Le ...been a millionaire he would no ...artyr of contemporary art. For ...d as reactionary and Conven... ...nkers of the day long excluded ...d by all. Through his life and ...hat individual courage is the ...ejudice.

...ort to reach out to most of his ...many years he was a close ...Lucian Freud, although he ...with Mr. Freud, Leon Kossoff, ...Kitaj and Michael Andrews in ...London. He also dismissed ...lem de Kooning and made no ...aste for the whole range of ...t movements.

...rest in this exhibition is that ...mated his "Three Studies for ...Crucifixion" in 1944, Bacon ...a vision of art. And until his ...of 83 he continued to explore ...d images of the human face ...ak his work from anything ...was subject in his later years ...friend to whom he left $16.9 ...member the 1944 triptych,

...with its monstrous semi-human figures set against an acid orange background, as marking the start of his career as an artist. In truth, he began drawing and painting more than 15 years earlier, but he destroyed almost everything he did. Of 10 surviving pre-1944 paintings, three are in the show here, including his ghostly "Crucifixion" of 1933, which was well received at the time.

Bacon was born in Dublin of English parents in 1909 and moved with his family to London in 1914. In 1925, at 16, he left home after a fight with his father and began what became an infamously bohemian life. He began work as a decorator and furniture designer and often went to Europe. In 1928, he visited a Picasso exhibition in Paris that inspired him to start drawing.

By the mid 1930's, he had given up decorating for

Bacon was a figurative painter in a sea of abstract and Conceptual artists.

painting but had had little success. He showed his work in some collective exhibitions and did odd jobs to make ends meet. The two other early works on display here point the way to his blazing use of rich, almost garish colors, although their styles are derivative. "Interior of a Room" (1935) of post-Cubism and "Figures in a Garden" (1936) of surrealism. Two of the works on paper, one an hommage to Picasso, also date to this period.

In 1944, recognition of Bacon as an original began to grow. His personal life was tumultuous: he was an inveterate gambler, he always drank heavily and he flaunted his homosexuality. But his provocative way of life seemed to inspire him to create. He was an avowed atheist, yet he returned frequently to the theme of crucifixion, always calling his works "studies," as if one day he planned to paint a complete

Continued on Page C20

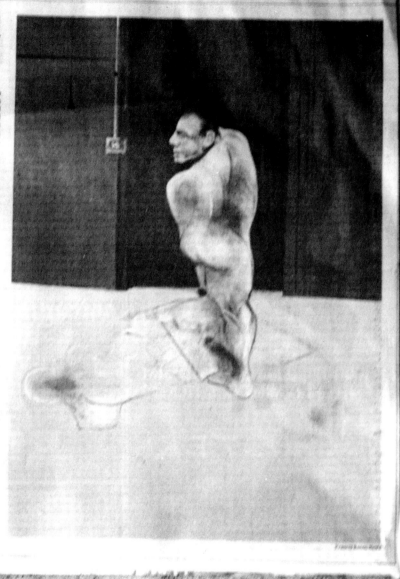

Francis Bacon's "Study for a Portrait of John Edwards" (1985), who was the artist's favorite subject in his final years and whom he left $16.9 million when he died in 1992.

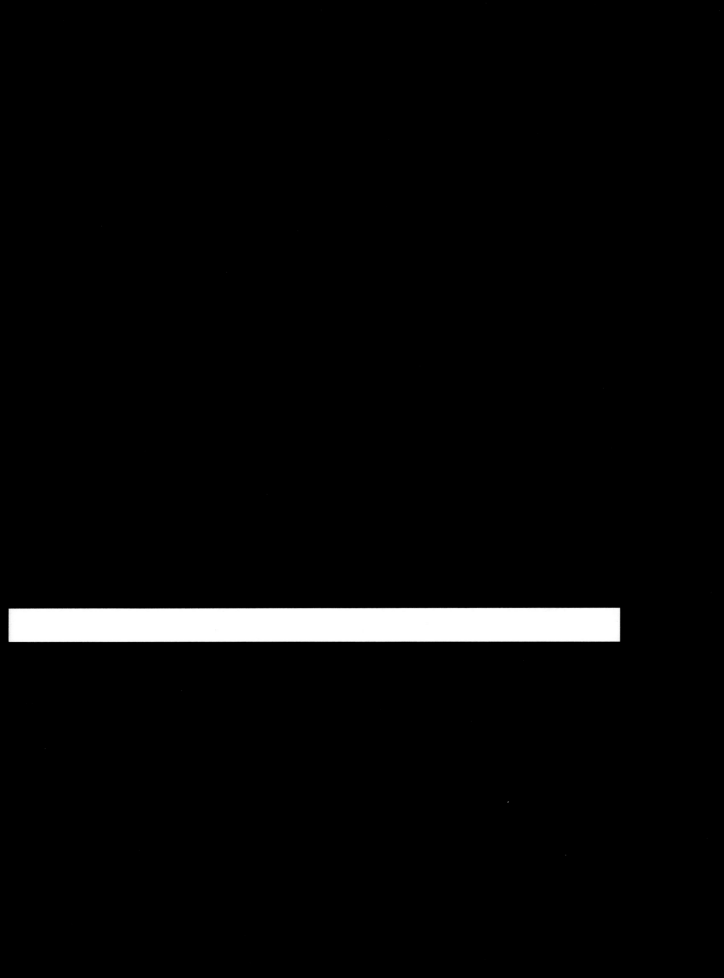

DD&D III

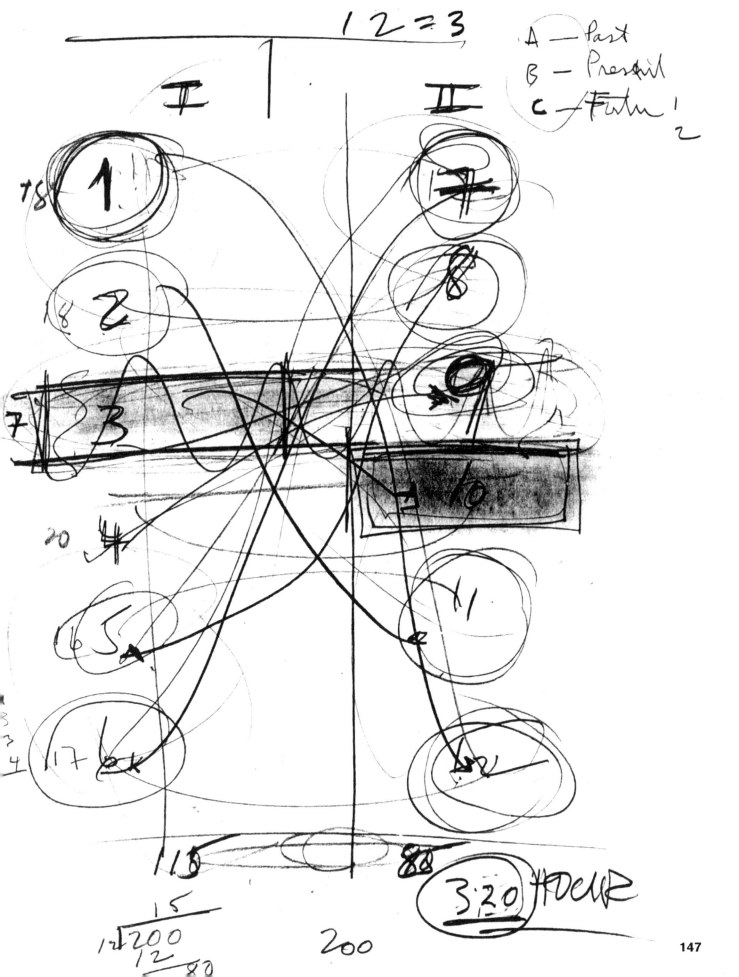

WEEKLY WORLD

NEWS

THE WORLD'S FOUR
GREATEST PROPHETS IN
ONE INCREDIBLE ISSUE!

FINAL

CHRIST · EDGAR · BILLY GRAHAM · NOSTRADAMUS

JESUS CAYCE

- REVEALED: Nuclear war erupts in Holy Land!
- REVEALED: Secret identity of the Anti-Christ!
- REVEALED: Exact date world will end

unbeliever, the triumphant return of Christ will prove disastrous — for Christ's return ensures final judgment.

"I have become more deeply aware of the enormous problems that face our world today and the dangerous trends which seem to be leading our world to the brink of Armageddon.

"I hear the approaching distant horsemen," he continued. "I hear their warnings and have no choice but to deliver them."

EDGAR CAYCE: The 20th century's foremost psychic foresaw horror and heartache for mankind and the world as

we approach the year beginning with devastating earthquakes, world war, holocaust, global epidemic, famine and finally, the end of life as we have known it.

Like Dr. Billy Graham and Christ himself, however, the news from Cayce isn't all bad. In a series of predictions that were kept secret until he foresaw the return of Christ shortly after the world went to apocalyptic warfare Dec. 31, 1999.

And he believed that Christ would usher in a era of perfect peace, happiness just as the Bible promised.

After a series of devastating earthquakes, said Cayce, world drought and horrible epidemics will kill hundreds of millions of people, and a massive hole in the ozone layer will open up over Earth, causing a terrifying

precedented plague of skin cancer, killing many millions more.

In 1999, continued the seer, Iraqi madman Saddam Hussein attacks Israel with nuclear missiles, prompting U.S. intervention and the beginning of World War III.

During this war a powerful and evil alliance led by Red China defeats a Western alliance led by the U.S.

In the fulfillment of Bible prophecy, a Chinese Anti-Christ identified as Min Lee forces people to forsake religion and wear the "mark of the beast," the evil number 666, on their hands.

On Dec. 31, 1999, the world ends. Within minutes, Christ returns to Earth — creating Heaven on Earth, Cayce said.

CHRIST: Most people think Jesus Christ merely hinted about the end of the

world when, in fact, he astonishingly specific — indirectly named the year 1999!

In the Bible itself, Matthew 24:4, Christ was quoted as having said:

"This gospel of the kingdom will be preached in the whole world as a testimony to all nations — and then the end will come."

That puts mankind well in the End Times, because the first and only time in history the gospel is being preached on a global scale via radio, television and print media.

Less than a year ago, Billy Graham preached to every nation on Earth simultaneously via satellite, essentially bringing the Word of God to every every man, woman and child with access to a radio or television.

And that's not all.

MUS

...covery of an ancient
...ll that contained what
...olars believe to be the
...st prophecies of Christ
...ven more specific than
... that.

...he scroll speaks of the
... of Satan in the West," a
...rence that suggests
...rica will be home to an
...Anti-Christ who will over...
... the genocide of Chris...
...e and touch off world war
...re Christ returns to...

...he prophecy dates the
... as occurring during the
...set of the second millen-
...," which most scholars
...eve is a clear reference to
... year 1999.

... the Bible points out.
...at will eventually estab-
... Paradise — the Kingdom
...od — on Earth and reign
... a perfect world for ster...

JESUS CHRIST

REVEALED: Exact date world will END!

...certainly no reason to stick
your head in the sand and hide.

"These prophecies, if you
choose to believe them, can
help you prepare for the end,
whether that means getting
right with God or running wild
in the streets with no regard
for a tomorrow that, quite
frankly, isn't going to come.

"In that regard, all of us face
deep and crucial moral and
ethical decisions. How will we
approach the end — with faith
and dignity or as wild animals?
That is for each of us to de-
cide."

Rachele's book is controver-
sial to say the least, but he not
only refuses to enter the de-
bate, he offers up hardly any

REVEREND
Dr. Billy
Graham.

...seer Nostradamus.

defense against his many ...
...es.

"I didn't write this book t...
win a popularity contest —...
wrote it to warn mankind o...
pending doom after stu...
the writings and comme...
of the greatest prophets ...
world has ever known," ...
plained Rachele.

"As for the accuracy of ...
work, I can only say that ...
don't believe me, go to ...
sources — the Bible is ...
them — and see for your...

Selections from Rache...
book follow on these ...
References to the Four ...
men of the Apocalypse in ...
Billy Graham's segment ...
to the symbolic harbing...
death and destruction ...
Bible's book of Revel...

NOSTRADAM...

The famed 16th...
...tury seer, p...
the greatest p...
the world has
known, flatly ...
that the world ...
end in a nuclear...
...caust on Dec. 31...
or Jan. 13, 200...
pending on who is ...
...preting the prophecy.
Included in his
Centuries and in indepe...
predictions that have bee...

...AL
...IES

...ntury!

REVEALED: Anti-...
millions of Chi...

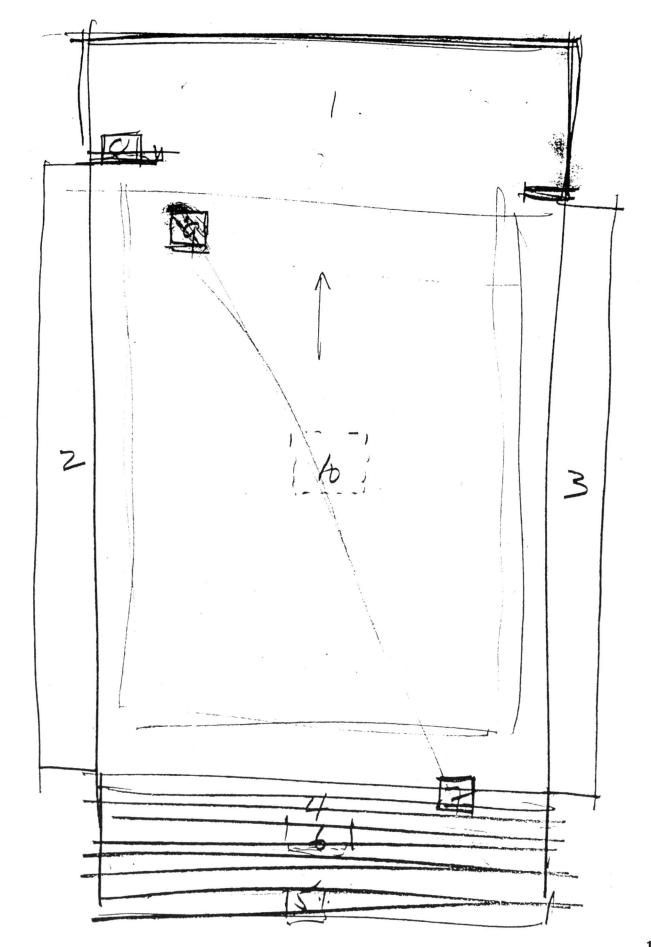

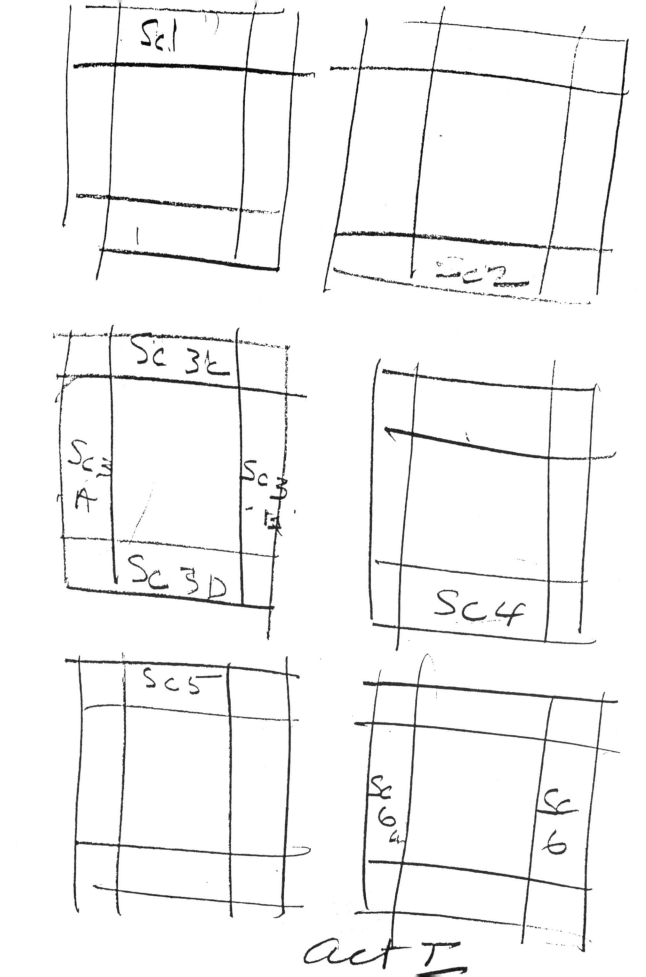

Sc.1

Sc 2

Sc 3℃

Sc 3
A

Sc 3
E

Sc 3D

Sc 4

Sc 5

Sc 6

Sc 6

act I

154

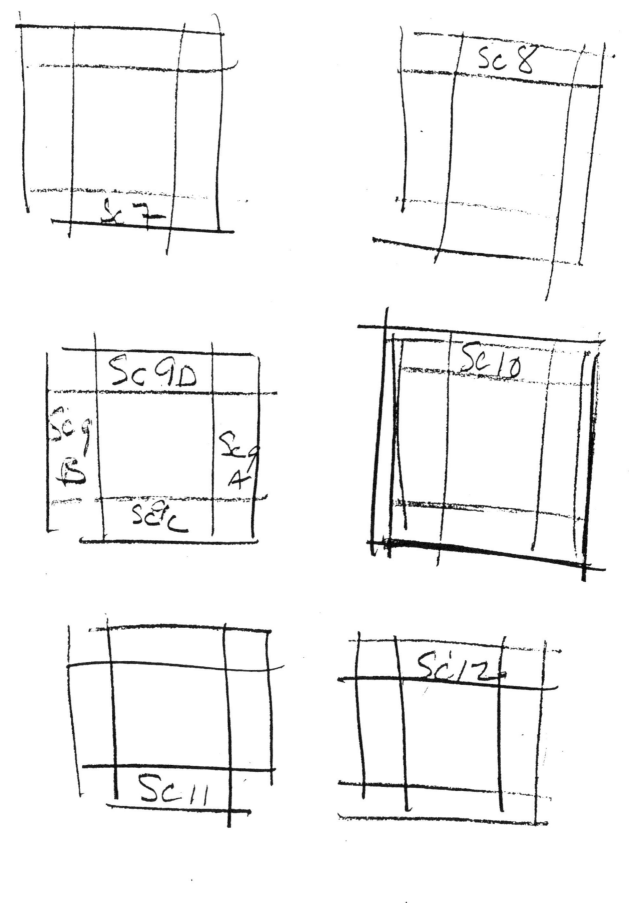

Sc 7

Sc 8

Sc 9D

Sc 9 B

Sc 9 A

Sc 9 C

Sc 10

Sc 11

Sc 12

act II

manners and conduct. He was the propagator of the Rule to such an extent that all the more important monasteries of Italy and Gaul, from Benevento to the Ocean, rejoiced to submit to his command. After his death Aymar succeeded him. He was a straightforward man who, although not so famous, was no less trusty a guardian of the observance of the Rule. After him the holy and venerable Mayol, whom we have already mentioned, was elected and he chose Odilo to lead the monks after him. He was the fourth abbot of Cluny after the founder Berno.[1] From this house brethren were frequently called out into many provinces, where they were set in authority as abbots and won much profit for the Lord. Father William, with whom this present chapter was begun, turned out to be a more industrious labourer and a more fruitful sower of the Rule than anyone who had gone from that house before him.

vi. *Holy relics found everywhere*

19. When the whole world was, as we have said, clothed in a white mantle of new churches, a little later, in the eighth year after the millennium of the Saviour's Incarnation, the relics of many saints were revealed by various signs where[2] they had long lain hidden. It was as though they had been waiting for a brilliant resurrection and were now by God's permission revealed to the gaze of the faithful; certainly they brought much comfort to men's minds. This revelation is known to have begun in the city of Sens in Gaul in the church of the holy martyr Stephen. The archbishop of that place was Lierri.[3] Wonderful to relate, he discovered there many ancient and holy things which had long lain hidden, amongst them a fragment of the staff of Moses. News of this discovery brought numbers of the faithful, not just from the provinces of Gaul but from most of Italy and the lands beyond the sea; no small number of them were sick people who returned, cured by the intervention of

[3] Lierri, archbishop of Sens, who was probably elected in 999 (*Odorannus*, p. 9), died in 1032: so the *Chronicon Sancti Petri Vivi*, p. 116, which also records (p. 108) that in the lifetime of Abbot Raynard of Saint-Pierre-de-Sens, who died in 1015 (and the context suggests actually in that year), Lierri searched for and found the long-lost relics of SS Savinianus and Potentianus. Healings and other miracles followed at their tombs. The 'invention' of relics was a growth industry in this period. Glaber records in the *Life*, c. viii, that when William rebuilt the abbey of Saint-Bénigne he found the long-lost tomb of the patron saint. The forging of relics, as recorded by Glaber below, 4. iii. 6, was a natural consequence of the cult. On the importance of the cult of relics see above, pp. lxix-lxx.

MOBY DICK by Herman Melville

Epilogue

"And I only am escaped alone to tell thee."
Job

THE drama's done. Why then here does any one step forth?—
Because one did survive the wreck.

It so chanced, that after the Parsee's disappearance, I was he
whom the Fates ordained to take the place of Ahab's bowsman,
when that bowsman assumed the vacant post; the same, who, when
on the last day the three men were tossed from out the rocking
boat, was dropped astern. So, floating on the margin of the ensu-
ing scene, and in full sight of it, when the half-spent suction of the
sunk ship reached me, I was then, but slowly, drawn towards the
closing vortex. When I reached it, it had subsided to a creamy pool.
Round and round, then, and ever contracting towards the button-
like black bubble at the axis of that slowly wheeling circle, like
another Ixion I did revolve. Till, gaining that vital centre, the
black bubble upward burst; and now, liberated by reason of its
cunning spring, and, owing to its great buoyancy, rising with
great force, the coffin life-buoy shot lengthwise from the sea, fell
over, and floated by my side. Buoyed up by that coffin, for almost
one whole day and night, I floated on a soft and dirge-like main.
The unharming sharks, they glided by as if with padlocks on their
mouths; the savage sea-hawks sailed with sheathed beaks. On the
second day, a sail drew near, nearer, and picked me up at last. It
was the devious-cruising Rachel, that in her retracing search after
her missing children, only found another orphan.

164

FINIS

The Velocity of the Mind

Watermill Center is a contemplative arcade where all kinds of different things can happen. We are formal and we are free. People come here to initiate ideas, to create and then go back out into the world.

Robert Wilson

Last summer we went to the Watermill Center to begin to work on this book with Robert Wilson. Two other passengers got off the train at Southhampton that evening. As the noisy train left, mist swirled up around us. After a three hour ride from Penn Station in Manhattan, the silence was comforting. We called the Center. A woman in a car came to fetch us. We pretended to have met her before. "Where could this have possibly been?" she demanded fiercely.

The first room we entered was lit by a bare bulb hanging on a wire from the ceiling. Some people were walking seemingly with no design through the space. At our left on a table was a fax machine. A fax was just coming in.

Wilson founded the Watermill Center in 1992 on Long Island, New York, as an international facility for the creation of new work. Every summer young artists from various countries meet Wilson in order to collaborate on projects. They all have different backgrounds such as theater, performance, sculpture, architecture, photography, video or sound-environment.

... a formal way of looking at a door of a refrigerator or at a dark grey TV triggers the implosion of the known and the remembered. It discloses an undefined space. Some aspects of Wilson's work familiar by now – the architecture in light, the mechanizing of human figures, the dissolving boundaries, limitless spaces and endless time or a logic that holds more similarities with dreaming than waking – seem to converge in the endeavor to broaden the perception of phenomena. We tried to make this point palpable within the confines of this book rather than to attend to pure documentation or to provide a report on the site.

Wilson's theater seems to be transient and fugitive. This transience mirrors the flux of consciousness. In looking at Wilson's performances the viewer engenders his or her own relation to space and time, to language and history. The pacing of images, the repetition of sounds carry the viewer beyond that point where knowledge becomes still, even a hindrance. You do not only relate to images seen and sounds heard, but also to images and sounds seen and heard before. They recur again, but differently, appearing within alternating configurations. They do not exactly repeat themselves, they rather insist. And it is this space in between that engenders an experience. Ezra Pound wrote: "To measure the duration of an experience, you must know the velocity of the mind."

The book itself is a field of images, in which the documentary and the imaginary, history and presence are elements of an expanded perception. It portrays a segment of time in which something always seems about to happen. It includes sketches, drawings, diagrams and texts for various projects by Wilson that were developed at the Watermill Center in the summer of 1996. The photographs do not relate to the plays or projects in an illustrative manner. They mirror the concrete site and the spatial and temporal conditions of experience. They highlight the interweaving of what could appear to be disparate and disconnected.

Sebastian Lohse & Vittorio Santoro
Zurich, June 1997

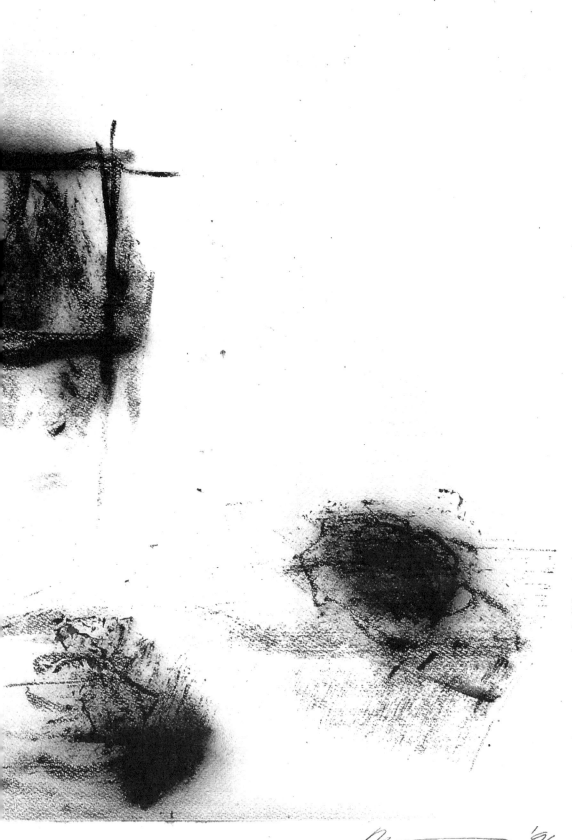

'96

ORLANDO was originally created in 1989 for the German actress Jutta Lampe and the *Schaubühne* in Berlin. Wilson, German dramaturge Wolfgang Wiens and British author Darryl Pinckney (collaborator on THE FOREST 1988 and TIME ROCKER 1996) adapted Virginia Woolf's novel about Orlando, a man of the court of Elizabeth I, who shifts lives and gender through the time and returns home at the beginning of the 20th century. In 1993, Isabelle Huppert took over the title role in a French production touring Switzerland, France, Italy, Portugal and Belgium. At the Watermill workshop in 1996 Wilson recreated the monologue with British actress Miranda Richardson for performances at the *Edinburgh Festival* in August 1996.

MONSTERS OF GRACE is a new kind of opera, a drama created by the separation of visual and musical architecture, of technical and human elements. The stage will be a space for purely visual constructions, for light and sculpture, projections and screens. Singers and voices in the orchestra pit will sing and speak texts which could be by the Dada poets Jean Arp and Kurt Schwitters or by Sufi poets. The title alludes to Hamlet's cry upon seeing the ghost of his father: "Angels and ministers of grace defend us!" The opening of MONSTERS OF GRACE is scheduled for May 1998 at UCLA's *Royce Hall* in Los Angeles. It marks a new development in Wilson's collaboration with Philip Glass, the composer of EINSTEIN ON THE BEACH (1976), the Rome section of THE CIVIL warS (1984) and the score for T.S.E. and for the DEATH OF MOLIERE film (1994).

The VILLA STUCK INSTALLATION was commissioned by the historic *Villa Stuck* in Munich for its centennial. In November 1997, Wilson will stage scenes from the life and art of the Bavarian painter, sculptor and architect Franz von Stuck (1863-1928), using life-size figures, props, light and photography. There will be installations in all living and working spaces of the ornate house based purely on Stuck's aesthetics and imagery, among them Stuck and his wife dressed as Romans and the restaged painting "The fantasy hunt." A score by Peter Cerone with sounds, music and texts will accompany the installation.

With THE LADY FROM THE SEA, Wilson will create a second solo for a great actress. Susan Sontag (whose play ALICE IN BED Wilson premiered in 1993 in Berlin) and dramaturge Wolfgang Wiens adapted the Ibsen play during the Watermill workshop 1996. The project will incorporate original music by Balinese musician Wayan Sudarsana and American composer Charles Winkler. French actress Dominique Sanda, who worked with Wilson in the silent prologue to Stravinsky's OEDIPUS REX (1996), will perform the monologue. The production is to premiere in Ferrara, Italy, in May 1998 and then tour Switzerland, France, and Japan.

DEATH, DESTRUCTION & DETROIT III is a coproduction of the New York *Lincoln Center Festival*, the festival of the European Cultural Capital 1999, the *Kunstfest Weimar*, the *Theater der Welt* festival/*Hebbel Theater*, Berlin, and the *Schaubühne*. Wilson already created two works called DEATH, DESTRUCTION & DETROIT, the first (1979) about Rudolf Hess, the second (1987) about Franz Kafka, both for the *Schaubühne*. The third part, which will premiere in 1999, focuses on the changing of times. During the Watermill workshop 1996 it was decided to set the work at the turn of the first millennium and to use texts and images from Western history to explore apocalyptic thought, history and its process of construction and destruction. DD&D III is composed of 12 scenes in two acts, and will be 3 hours and 20 minutes in length. Like DD&D II, the new work will run on four parallel stages enclosing the audience in the center.

Wilson's plan to work on Luigi Nono's *tragedia dell'ascolto* PROMETEO dates back to an encounter in Berlin in the mid-eighties, when the Italian composer said that Wilson would probably be the only one capable of staging this unstageable work for two conductors, vocal and instrumental soloists, a choir and an orchestra, two speakers and a complex system of live electronics. Sponsored by the Brussels opera, Wilson created his *mise en espace* in March 1997 in the *Halles de Schaerbeek*, adding an installation and an abstract choreography for young dancers developed in a Watermill workshop.

List of works

Quotations from written texts such as *Orlando* are cited here in selected shortened versions, while play sketches and diagrams have also been only sampled.

All photographs *Untitled*, 1996. They were taken in Watermill, Long Island, and in New York City.

Acknowledgements

Orlando by Virginia Woolf. Adapted for the stage by Darryl Pinckney, Wolfgang Wiens and Robert Wilson © 1989.

Konfiguration I by Hans Arp from Hans Arp, *Worte mit und ohne Anker*. Published by Limes Verlag, Wiesbaden 1957.

The Louse and the Flea by Jakob and Wilhelm Grimm from *Grimm's Tales for Young and Old*. Translation by Ralph Manheim © Doubleday, New York 1977. Printed here with the kind permission of Doubleday, New York.

introduction to max ernst's natural history by Hans Arp from Jean Arp, *On My Way: Poetry and Essays 1912-1947*. Wittenborn, Schultz, Inc., New York 1948.

Four Bear Songs, No. 3 by Kurt Schwitters from Kurt Schwitters, *Poems, Performances, Pieces, Proses, Plays, Poetics*. Edited and translated by Jerôme Rothenberg and Pierre Joris © Temple University Press, Philadelphia 1993. Printed here with the kind permission of Temple University Press, Philadelphia.

The Ditmarsh Tale of Lies by Jakob and Wilhelm Grimm from *Grimm's Tales for Young and Old*. Translation by Ralph Manheim © Doubleday, New York 1977. Printed here with the kind permission of Doubleday, New York.

Excerpts from **Odes** by Jelaluddin Rumi from Jelaluddin Rumi, *Open Secret*. Translated by John Moyne-Coleman Barks © Threshold Books, Putney, Vermont, 1984.

Scene from **The Lady From The Sea** by Susan Sontag (based on the play by Henrik Ibsen) © 1997 by Susan Sontag. Printed here with the kind permission of Susan Sontag.

Excerpt from **Holy Relics Found Everywhere** by Rodulfus Glaber from Rodulfus Glaber, *The Five Books of Histories*. Edited and translated by John France © Clarendon Press, Oxford 1989.

Excerpt from **Moby Dick** by Herman Melville © W.W. Norton Company, Inc., New York & London 1967.

Liner notes to Tea and Sympathy by Jan Linders.

We apologize for the possible omission of credits as not all sources or current copyright holders could be identified and confirmed before printing.

The publishers wish to express their deepest gratitude to Konstantin Rossowsky for his generous support.
Thanks go to Richard E. Fitzgerald, Arina Kowner, Jan Linders, Jos Näpflin, Annemarie Verna, Geoffrey Wexler/Byrd Hoffman Foundation, New York and Ilford (Suisse).
Special thanks to Sonja Bachmann and Wolfgang Wiens/Thalia Theater, Hamburg, for their invaluable textual research.

The stay of Sebastian Lohse and Vittorio Santoro at Watermill was made possible by a generous grant from Migros Kulturprozent and supported by Swissair.

Published by MEMORY/CAGE EDITIONS
P.O.Box 1923
Zurich/Switzerland
T/F (41 1) 241 04 45

Conceived and edited by Sebastian Lohse & Vittorio Santoro
Designed by Vittorio Santoro & Robert Wilson
Production by Daniel Kurjaković
Color separation by Salinger AG, Zurich
Printed in Switzerland by Druckerei Robert Hürlimann AG, Zurich

First printing

There is a special limited edition of 25 copies of this book including a collotype especially created for this project. Each collotype is signed by Robert Wilson. The collotypes were printed by item editions, Paris, in May 1997, and are numbered as follows: 1/25 - 25/25 with 10 H.C.

Distributed in the U.S. by D.A.P. (Distributed Art Publishers), New York, N.Y., Telephone (212) 627.1999

ISBN 3-9520497-6-X